Big Data Analyt

Big Data Analytics

Editor

Dr A M Viswa Bharathy, B.E., M.E., Ph.D., MISTE, MIEI,
Professor, School of Computer Science and Engineering,
Malla Reddy College of Engineering and Technology,
Hyderabad, India.

Authors

Dr V Chandrasekar, B.E., M.E., M.B.A., Ph.D.,
Professor, School of Computer Science and Engineering,
Malla Reddy College of Engineering and Technology,
Hyderabad, India.

Ms V Shanmugavalli, B.E., M.E., (Ph.D.),
Assistant Professor,
Department of Computer Science and Engineering,
KSR College of Engineering,
Tamil Nadu, India.

CWP

Central West Publishing

This edition has been published by Central West Publishing, Australia

For more information about the books published by Central West Publishing, please visit https://centralwestpublishing.com

Disclaimer
Every effort has been made by the publisher, editor and authors while preparing this book, however, no warranties are made regarding the accuracy and completeness of the content. The publisher, editor and authors disclaim without any limitation all warranties as well as any implied warranties about sales, along with fitness of the content for a particular purpose. Citation of any website and other information sources does not mean any endorsement from the publisher and authors. For ascertaining the suitability of the contents contained herein for a particular lab or commercial use, consultation with the subject expert is needed. In addition, while using the information and methods contained herein, the practitioners and researchers need to be mindful for their own safety, along with the safety of others, including the professional parties and premises for whom they have professional responsibility. To the fullest extent of law, the publisher, editor and authors are not liable in all circumstances (special, incidental, and consequential) for any injury and/or damage to persons and property, along with any potential loss of profit and other commercial damages due to the use of any methods, products, guidelines, procedures contained in the material herein.

A catalogue record for this book is available from the National Library of Australia

ISBN (print): 978-1-922617-17-0

Dedicated to

My Family and Guide Dr S Suresh Kumar
- Dr V Chandrasekar

My Mom and Dad, for what I am now
and Wife for supporting me
- Dr A M Viswa Bharathy

My Family
- Ms V Shanmugavalli

Contents

Preface

The book serves as a perfect guide for those who aspire to learn big data analytics, algorithms and its tools. The book has been divided into five units, where in each unit focuses on an important aspect of big data. The first unit deals with the fundamentals of big data, challenges associated with it and various tools for analytics. The second unit deals with the different analytical approaches, popular tools and a guide for building a well-designed analytics team. The third unit elaborates the framework and architecture of MapReduce, HBase and fundamental concepts to understand the HDFS file system types and its commands. The fourth unit gives a detailed note on Hadoop and its applications, with a focus on managing resources on distributed computing environment. The fifth unit helps to understand the text mining process, social media analytics, mobile and web analytics and the tools for it. The book solves the purpose of being a guide to both academic and professional people. The concepts are well explained with neat diagrams and examples, wherever deemed necessary. There's no doubt that this book will be one of the best in its field.

We, the authors, are ever indebted to our college management and fellow faculty for having helped us in shaping the book to come out as it's now. We thank the publication team for accepting our book and publishing it under their arena.

UNIT 1

BIG DATA ANALYTICS

Now a days, companies have started to realize the importance of data availability in large amounts in order to make the right decisions and support their strategies. With the development of new technologies, the Internet and social networks, the production of digital data is constantly growing. The term "Big Data" refers to the heterogeneous mass of digital data produced by companies and individuals whose characteristics (large volume, different forms, speed of processing) require specific and increasingly sophisticated computer storage and analysis tools.

War is 90% information
Napoleon Bonaparte

1.1 Introduction

The digital data produced is partly the result of the use of devices connected to the Internet. Thus, smartphones, tablets and computers transmit data about their users. The connected smart objects convey information about the consumer's use of the everyday objects.

Apart from the connected devices, data come from a wide range of sources: demographic data, climate data, scientific and medical data, energy consumption data, etc. All these data provide information about the location of users of the devices, their travel, their interests, their consumption habits, their leisure activities, and their projects and so on. However, information on how the infrastructure, machinery and apparatus is also used.

With the ever-increasing number of Internet and mobile phone users, the volume of digital data is growing rapidly. Today we are living in an Informational Society and we are moving towards a Knowledge Based Society. In order to extract better knowledge, we need a bigger amount of data. The Society of Information is a society where information plays a major role at the economical, cultural and political stage.

The volume of data that one has to deal has exploded to unimaginable levels in the past decade, and at the same time, the price of data storage has systematically reduced. Private companies and research institutions capture terabytes of data about their users' interactions, business, social media, and also sensors from devices such as mobile phones and automobiles. The challenge of this era is to make sense of this sea of data. This is where big data analytics comes into picture.

Data

The quantities, characters, or symbols on which operations are performed by a computer, which may be stored and transmitted in the form of electrical signals and recorded on magnetic, optical, or mechanical recording media

Definition of Big data

The term "Big Data" refers to the evolution and use of technologies that provide the right user at the right time with the right information from a mass of data that has been growing exponentially for a long time in our society. The challenge is not only to deal with rapidly increasing volumes of data, but also the difficulty of managing increasingly heterogeneous formats as well as increasingly complex and interconnected data.

Big Data is also data but with a huge size. Big Data is a term used to describe a collection of data that is huge in size and yet growing exponentially with time.

In short, such data is so large and complex that none of the traditional data management tools are able to store it or process it efficiently.

1.1.1 Examples of Big Data

1. The New York Stock Exchange generates about one terabyte of new trade data per day.
2. The statistic shows that 500+terabytes of new data get ingested into the databases of social media site Facebook, every day. This data is mainly generated in terms of photo and video uploads, message exchanges, putting comments etc.
3. A single Jet engine can generate 10+terabytes of data in 30 minutes of flight time. With many thousand flights per day, generation of data reaches upto many Petabytes.

The term Big Data refers to a huge volume of data that cannot be stored processed by any traditional data storage or processing units. Big Data is generated at a very large scale and it is being used by many multinational companies to process and analyse in order to uncover insights and improve the business of many organisations.

However, there are certain basic tenets of Big Data that will make it even simpler to answer what is Big Data:

1. It refers to a massive amount of data that keeps on growing exponentially with time.

2. It is so voluminous that it cannot be processed or analyzed using conventional data processing techniques.
3. It includes data mining, data storage, data analysis, data sharing, and data visualization.
4. The term is an all-comprehensive one including data, data frameworks, along with the tools and techniques used to process and analyze the data.

1.1.2 Elements and Types of Big Data

As you have learned 'What is Big Data?', it is important to understand how can data be categorized as Big Data? For that, we have five Vs:

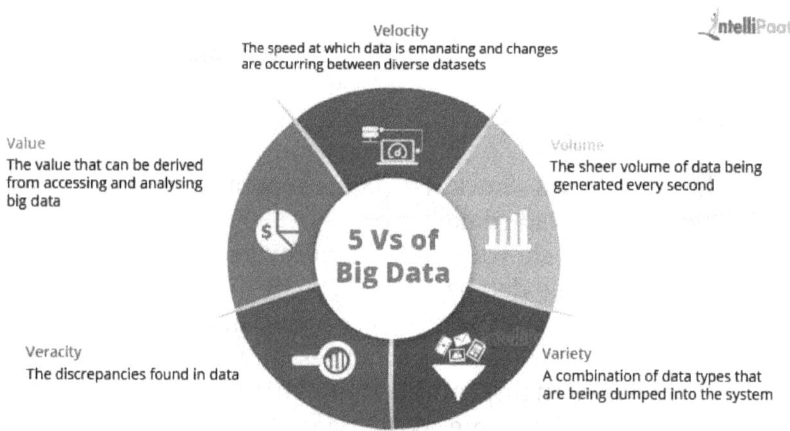

1. Volume: This refers to the data that is tremendously large. As you can see from the image, the volume of data is rising exponentially. In 2016, the data created was only 8 ZB and it is expected that, by 2020, the data would rise up to 40 ZB, which is extremely large.

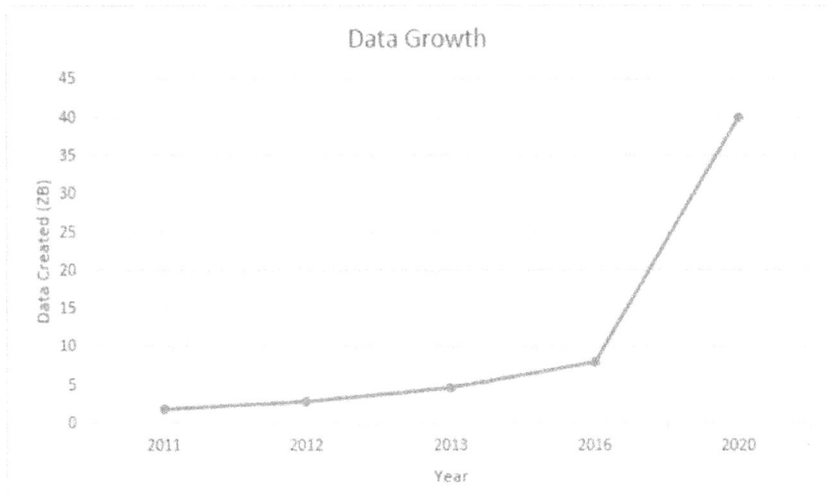

2. Variety: A reason for this rapid growth of data volume is that the data is coming from different sources in various formats. The data is categorized as follows:

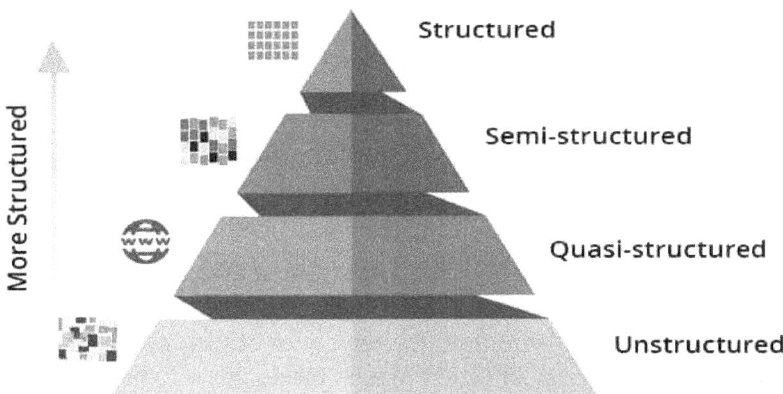

a) Structured Data: Here, data is present in a structured schema, along with all the required columns. It is in a structured or tabular format. Data that is stored in a relational database management system is an example of structured data. For example, in the below-given employee table, which is present in a database, the data is in a structured format.

Emp ID	Emp Name	Gender	Department	Salary
2383	ABC	Male	Finance	6,50,000
4623	XYZ	Male	Admin	50,00,000

b) Semi-structured Data: In this form of data, the schema is not properly defined, i.e., both forms of data is present. So, basically semi-structured data has a structured form but it isn't defined, e.g., JSON, XML, CSV, TSV, and email. The web application data that is unstructured contains transaction history files, log files, etc. OLTP systems (Online Transaction Processing) are built to work with structured data and the data is stored in relations, i.e., tables.

Example: XML file

```
<product>
<name>Pen </name>
<price>$7.95</price>
</product>
<product>
<name>Paper </name>
<price>$8.95</price>
</product>
```

c) Unstructured Data: In this data format, all the unstructured files such as video files, log files, audio files, and image files are included. Any data which has an unfamiliar model or structure is categorized as unstructured data. Since the size is large, unstructured data possesses various challenges in terms of processing for deriving value out of it. An example for this is a complex data source that contains a blend of text files, videos, and images. Several organizations have a lot of data available with them but these organizations don't know how to derive value out of it since the data is in its raw form.

Example: Output returned by **'Google Search'**

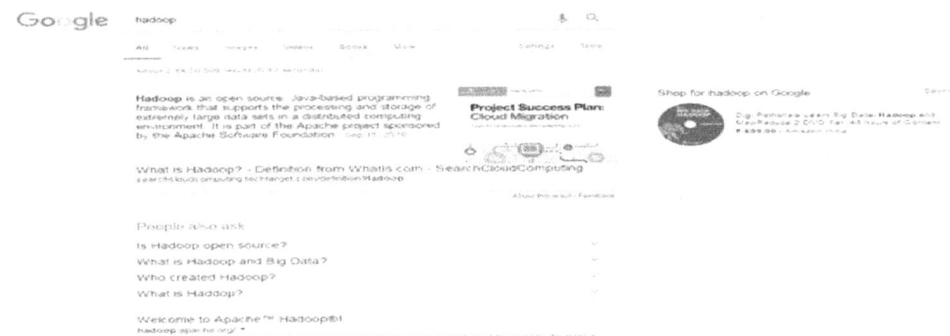

d) Quasi-structured Data: This data format consists of textual data with inconsistent data formats that can be formatted with effort and time, and with the help of several tools. For example, web server logs, i.e., a log file that is automatically created and maintained by some server which contains a list of activities.

3. Velocity: The speed of data accumulation also plays a role in determining whether the data is categorized into big data or normal data. As can be seen from the image below, at first, mainframes were used wherein fewer people used computers. Then came the client/server model and more and more computers were evolved. After this, the web applications came into the picture and started increasing over the Internet. Then, everyone began using these applications. These applications were then used by more and more devices such as mobiles as they were very easy to access. Hence, a lot of data! As it is clear from the image, every 60 seconds, so much of the data is generated.

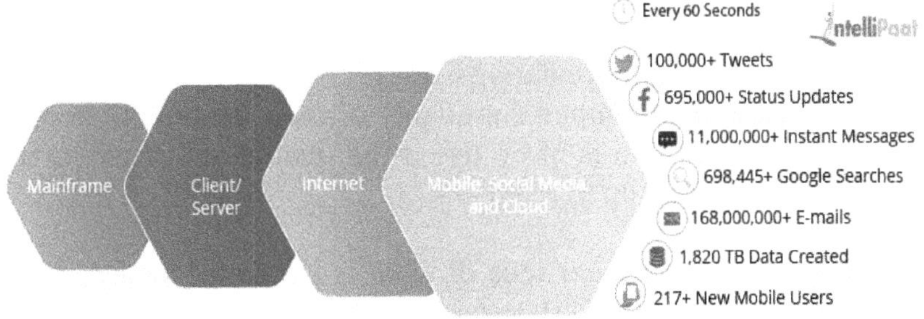

4. Value: How will the extraction of data work? Here, our fourth V comes in, which deals with a mechanism to bring out the correct meaning out of data. First of all, you need to mine the data, i.e., a process to turn raw data into useful data. Then, an analysis is done on the data that you have cleaned or retrieved out of the raw data. Then, you need to make sure whatever analysis you have done benefits your business such as in finding out insights, results, etc. which were not possible earlier.

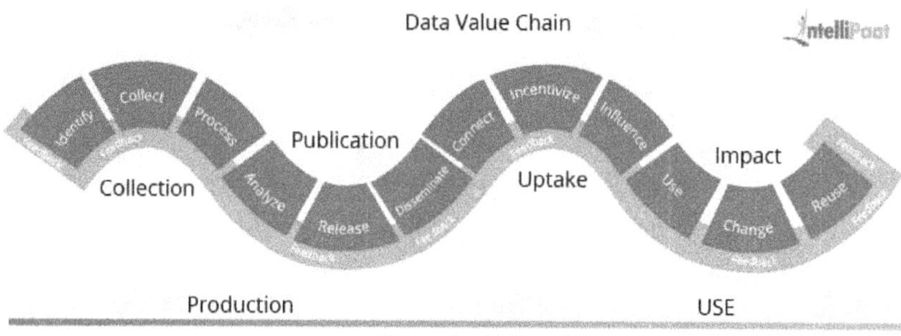

You need to make sure that whatever raw data you are given, you have cleaned it to be used for deriving business insights. After you have cleaned the data, a challenge pops up, i.e., during the process of dumping a huge amount of data, some packages might have lost. So for resolving this issue, our next V comes into the picture.

5. Veracity: Since the packages get lost during the execution, we need to start again from the stage of mining raw data in order to convert them into valuable data. And this process goes on. Also, there will be uncertainties and inconsistencies in the data. To overcome this, our last V comes into place, i.e., Veracity. Veracity means the trustworthiness and quality of data. It is necessary that the veracity of the data is maintained. For example, think about Facebook posts, with hashtags, abbreviations, images, videos, etc., which make them unreliable and hamper the quality of their content. Collecting loads and loads of data is of no use if the quality and trustworthiness of the data is not up to the mark.

Now, that you have a sheer idea of what is big data, let's check out the major sectors using Big Data on an everyday basis.

1.2 Difference Between Structured, Semi-structured and Unstructured Data

Factors	Structured data	Semi-structured data	Unstructured data
Flexibility	It is dependent and less flexible	It is more flexible than structured data but less than flexible than unstructured data	It is flexible in nature and there is an absence of a schema
Transaction Management	Matured transaction and various concurrency technique	The transaction is adapted from DBMS not matured	No transaction management and no concurrency
Query performance	Structured query allow complex joining	Queries over anonymous nodes are possible	An only textual query is possible
Technology	It is based on the relational database table	It is based on RDF and XML	This is based on character and library data

1.3 Major Sectors Using Big Data Every Day

Banking

As there is a massive amount of data that is gushing in from innumerable sources, banks need to find uncommon and unconventional ways in order to manage big data. It's also essential to examine customer requirements, render services according to their specifications, and reduce risks while sustaining regulatory compliance. Financial institutions have to deal with Big Data Analytics in order to solve this problem.

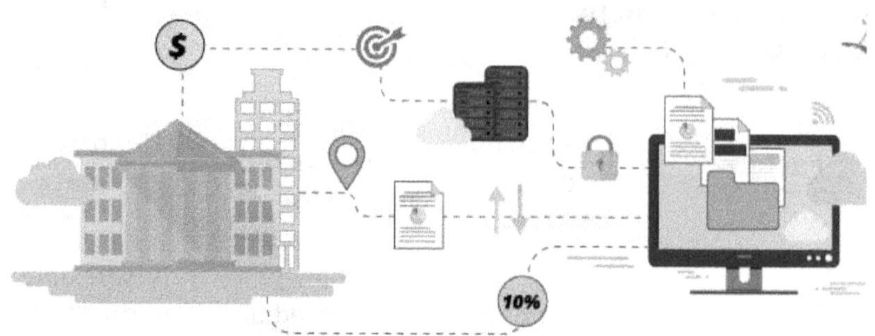

NYSE (New York Stock Exchange)

NYSE generates about one terabyte of new trade data every single day. Thus, imagine if one terabyte of data is generated every day, in a whole year how much data there would be to process. This is what Big Data is used for.

Government

Government agencies utilize Big Data and have devised a lot of running agencies, managing utilities, dealing with traffic jams, or limiting the effects of crime. However, apart from its benefits in Big Data, the government also addresses the concerns of transparency and privacy.

Aadhar Card

The Indian government has a record of all 1.21 billion citizens. This huge data is stored and analyzed to find out several things, such as the number of youths in the country. According to which several schemes are made to target the maximum population. All this big data can't be stored in some traditional database, so it is left for storing and analyzing using several Big Data Analytics tools.

Education

Education concerning Big Data produces a vital impact on students, school systems, and curriculums. With interpreting big data, people can ensure students' growth, identify at-risk students, and achieve an improvised system for the evaluation and assistance of principals and teachers.

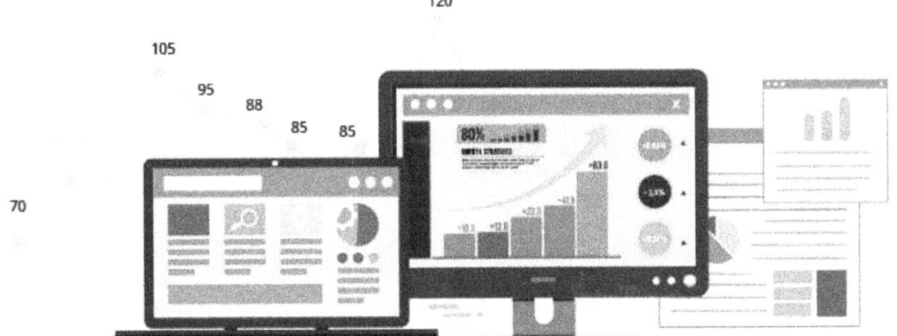

Example: The education sector holds a lot of information with regard to curriculum, students, and faculty. The information is analyzed to get insights that can enhance the operational adequacy of the educational organization. Collecting and analyzing information of a student such as attendance, test scores, grades, and other issues take up a lot of data. So, big data makes an approach for a progressive framework wherein this data can be stored and analyzed making it easier for the institutes to work with.

Big Data in Healthcare

When it comes to what Big Data is in Healthcare, we can see that it is being used enormously. It includes collecting data, analyzing it, leveraging it for customers. Also, patients' clinical data is too complex to be solved or understood by traditional systems. Since big data is processed by Machine Learning algorithms and Data Scientists, tackling such huge data becomes manageable.

Example: Nowadays, doctors rely mostly on patients' clinical records, which means that a lot of data needs to be gathered, that too for different patients. Obviously, it is not possible for old or traditional data storage methods to store this data. Since there is a large amount of data coming from different sources, in various formats, the need to handle this large amount of data is increased, and that is why the Big Data approach is needed.

E-commerce

Maintaining customer relationships is the most important in the e-commerce industry. E-commerce websites have different marketing ideas to retail their merchandise to their customers, to manage transactions, and to implement better tactics of using innovative ideas with Big Data to improve businesses.

Flipkart: Flipkart is a huge e-commerce website dealing with lots of traffic on a daily basis. But, when there is a pre-announced sale on Flipkart, traffic grows exponentially that actually crashes the website. So, to handle this kind of traffic and data, Flipkart uses Big Data. Big Data can actually help in organizing and analyzing the data for further use.

Social Media

Social media in the current scenario is considered as the largest data generator. The stats have shown that around 500+ terabytes of new data get generated into the databases of social media every day, particularly in the case of Facebook. The data generated mainly consist of videos, photos, message exchanges, etc. A single activity on any social media site generates a lot of data which is again stored and gets processed whenever required. Since the data stored is in terabytes, it would take a lot of time for processing if it is done by our legacy systems. Big Data is a solution to this problem.

Travel and Tourism

Travel and tourism are one of the biggest users of Big Data Technology. It has enabled us to predict the requirements for travel facilities in many places, improving business through dynamic pricing and many more.

1.4 Advantages of Big Data

Big Data Technology has given us multiple advantages, out of which we will now discuss a few.

1. Big Data has enabled predictive analysis which can save organizations from operational risks.
2. Predictive analysis has helped organizations grow business by analyzing customer needs.
3. Big Data has enabled many multimedia platforms to share data Ex: YouTube, Instagram
4. Medical and Healthcare sectors can keep patients under constant observations.
5. Big Data changed the face of customer-based companies and worldwide market.

1.5 Tools and Techniques

1. Artificial Intelligence (AI), IoT, and social media are driving the data complexity through new forms and sources. For ex-

ample, it is crucial that, in real time, big data coming through sensors, devices, networks, transaction is captured, managed, and processed with low latency.

2. Big Data enables analysts, researchers, and business users to make more informed decisions faster, using historic data which otherwise was unattainable.
3. One can use text analysis, machine learning, predictive analytics, data mining, and natural language processing to extract new insight from the available pile of data.
4. The technology has evolved to manage massive volumes of data, which previously were expensive and had to have the help of supercomputers.
5. With the emergence of social media like Facebook, search engines like Google, and Yahoo!, Big Data projects got impetus and grew as it is today.
6. Tech such as MapReduce, Hadoop, and Big Table have been developed to fulfill the today's need.
7. The NoSQL repositories are also mentioned in relation to Big Data. It is an alternate database in contrast to relational databases.
8. These databases do not organize records in tables of rows and columns as found in the conventional relational databases.
9. There are different types of NoSQL databases, such as Content Store, Document Store, Event Store, Graph, Key Value, and the like.
10. They do not use SQL for queries, and they follow a different architectural model. They are found to facilitate Big Data Analytics in a favorable manner.
11. Some popular names are: Hbase, MongoDB, CouchDB, and Neo4j. Apart from these, there are many others.

1.6 Introduction to Big Data Analytics

The volume of data that one has to deal has exploded to unimaginable levels in the past decade, and at the same time, the price of data storage has systematically reduced. Private companies and research institutions capture terabytes of data about their users' interactions, business, social media, and also sensors from devices such as mobile phones and automobiles. The challenge of this era is to make sense of this sea of data. This is where big data analytics comes in picture.

Analytics is an encompassing and multidimensional field. It uses mathematics, statistics, predictive modeling and machine-learning techniques to find meaningful patterns and knowledge in recorded data.

Big Data Analytics can be defined as a process of examining large and varied data sets. We use advanced analytics techniques against the large data to uncover the hidden patterns, unknown correlations, market trends, customer preferences, and other useful information.

Basically, Big Data Analytics is helping large companies facilitate their growth and development. And it majorly includes applying various data mining algorithms on a certain dataset. With the use of Big data analytics, one can make informed decisions without blindly relying on guesses.

Big Data Analytics largely involves collecting data from different sources, mange it in a way that it becomes available to be consumed by analysts and finally deliver data products useful to the organization business.

The process of converting large amounts of unstructured raw data, retrieved from different sources to a data product useful for organizations forms the core of Big Data Analytics.

1.6.1 History and Evolution of Big Data Analytics

The concept of big data has been around for years; most organizations now understand that if they capture all the data that streams into their businesses, they can apply analytics and get significant value from it. But even in the 1950s, decades before anyone uttered the term "big data," businesses were using basic analytics essentially numbers in a spreadsheet that were manually examined to uncover insights and trends.

The new benefits that big data analytics brings to the table, however, are speed and efficiency. A few years ago, a business would have gathered information, run analytics and unearthed information that could be used for future decisions. Today, the business can identify insights for immediate decisions.

1.6.2 How Does Big Data Analytics Work?

Numerous data are being generated every minute. As we all know social media sites and applications play the prime part in generating data. Massive amounts of data cannot be handled in traditional ways.

Hadoop is the solution to this problem. It is a framework that manages the distribution and processes of big data. Hadoop Distributed File System is the storage unit of Hadoop where data is divided and stored amongst many storage units.

Big Data has to be processed, stored and analyzed to put into effective use for businesses.

1.6.3 How is Big Data Analytics Used Today?

Big Data Analytics is used in a number of industries to allow organizations and companies to make better decisions, as well as verify and disprove existing theories or models. The focus of Data Analytics lies in inference, which is the process of deriving conclusions that are solely based on what the researcher already knows.

Let us now see a few of the Big Data Analytics tools.

1. **ApacheHadoop:** Big Data Hadoop is a framework that allows you to store big data in a distributed environment for parallel processing.
2. **Apache Pig:** Apache Pig is a platform that is used for analyzing large datasets by representing them as data flows. Pig is basically designed in order to provide an abstraction over MapReduce which reduces the complexities of writing a MapReduce program.
3. **Apache Base:** Apache HBase is a multidimensional, distributed, open-source, and NoSQL database written in Java. It runs on top of HDFS providing Bigtable-like capabilities for Hadoop.
4. **ApacheSpark:** Apache Spark is an open-source general-purpose cluster-computing framework. It provides an interface for programming all clusters with implicit data parallelism and fault tolerance.
5. **Talend:** Talend is an open-source data integration platform. It provides many services for enterprise application integration, data integration, data management, cloud storage, data quality, and Big Data.
6. **Splunk:** Splunk is an American company that produces software for monitoring, searching, and analyzing machine-generated data using a Web-style interface.
7. **Apache Hive:** Apache Hive is a data warehouse system developed on top of Hadoop and is used for interpreting structured and semi-structured data.
8. **Kafka:** Apache Kafka is a distributed messaging system that was initially developed at LinkedIn and later became part of the Apache project. Kafka is agile, fast, scalable, and distributed by design.

1.6.4 Benefits of Big Data Analytics

Big Data Analytics is indeed a revolution in the field of Information Technology. The use of Data Analytics by various companies is increasing every year. The primary focus of them is on their customers. Hence, the field is flourishing in Business-to-Consumer (B2C) applications.

Big data analytics is time-sensitive, used to take faster decision from huge amount of diversified data and used to find the deep and richer insights of the business. It is one kind of technology enabled analytics.

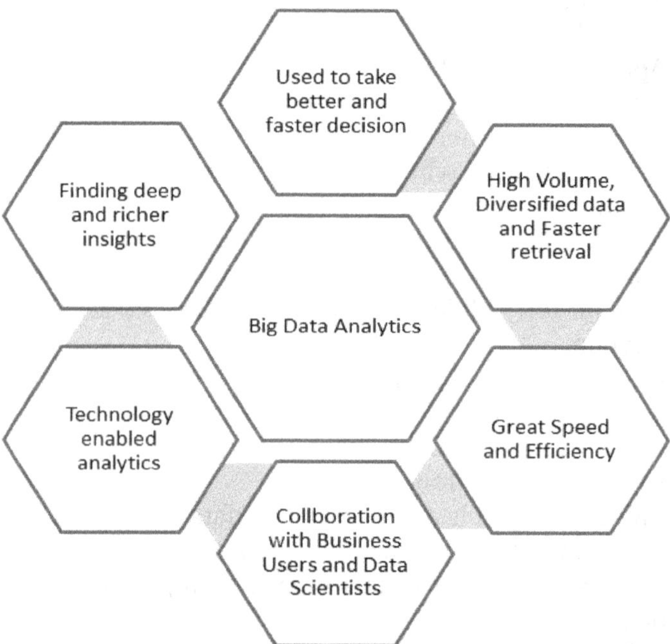

1.6.5 What Big Data Analytics Isn't

Big data analytics is not to replace the RDBMS or traditional data warehouse.

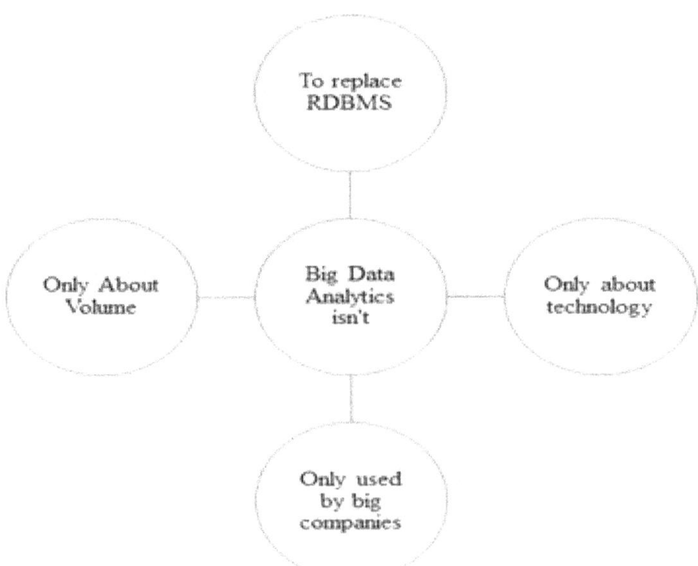

Big data analytics is co-existing with both RDBMS and Data Warehouse. If you have only huge amount of data then you cannot say that it is big data. Huge Volume is a characteristic, but only Volume cannot justify big data. It is not only used by big companies, it can be used by any company.

1.6.6 Classification of Analytics

For different stages of business analytics huge amount of data is processed at various steps. Depending on the stage of the workflow and the requirement of data analysis, there are four main kinds of analytics – descriptive, diagnostic, predictive and prescriptive. These four types together answer everything a company needs to know- from what's going on in the company to what solutions to be adopted for optimizing the functions.

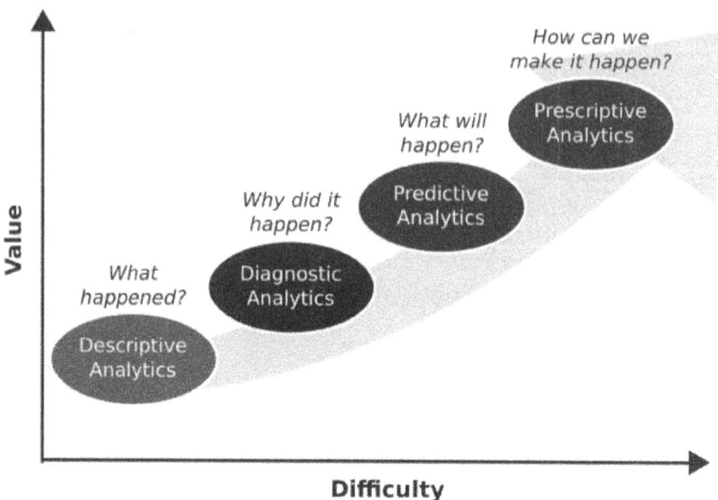

1. **Prescriptive Analysis:** Data analysis that provides answers to what actions should be taken.
2. **Predictive Analysis:** An analysis of data that can be used to predict what situation or number of situations may results.
3. **Diagnostic Analysis:** Data analysis that provides insight into what happened in the past and why.
4. **Descriptive Analysis:** Data analysis that can be real-time or leveraged to see what is currently happening.

1.6.7 Greatest Challenges Preventing Businesses from Capitalizing on Big Data

1. A research from Tata Consultancy Services among 1,217 companies about how companies invest in big data and derive results from it also revealed the 10 greatest challenges businesses face when implementing a big data strategy.
2. The research revealed that big data is clearly paying off for some companies, and big time in some cases. There are however also a lot of companies that face difficult challenges moving ahead with big data.
3. The below infographic lists the 10 most important challenges. A research from Tata Consultancy Services among 1,217 companies about how companies invest in big data and derive results from it also revealed the 10 greatest challenges businesses face when implementing a big data strategy.

4. The research revealed that big data is clearly paying off for some companies, and big time in some cases. There are however also a lot of companies that face difficult challenges moving ahead with big data.
5. The below infographic lists the 10 most important challenges. Interesting fact is that most of the challenges are cultural challenges and not so much the technical difficulties of big data.

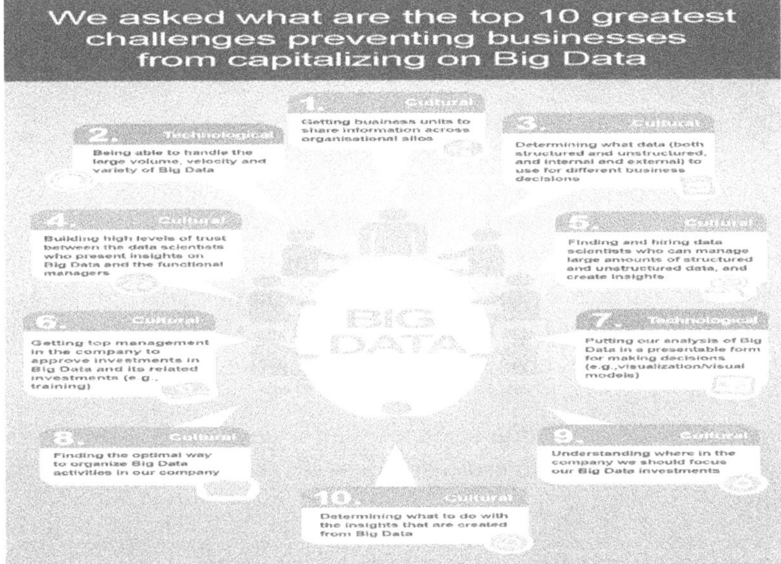

1.7 Data Science

Data science is complex and involves many specific domains and skills, but the general definition is that data science encompasses all the ways in which information and knowledge is extracted from data.

Data science is an evolutionary extension of statistics capable of dealing with the massive amounts of data produced today. It adds methods from computer science to the repertoire of statistics.

The main things that set a data scientist apart from a statistician are the ability to work with big data and experience in machine learning, computing, and algorithm building. Their tools tend to differ too, with data scientist job descriptions more frequently mentioning the ability to use Hadoop, Pig, Spark, R, Python, and Java, among others.

Python is a great language for data science because it has many data science libraries available, and it's widely supported by specialized software. For instance, almost every popular NoSQL database has a Python-specific API. Because of these features and the ability to prototype quickly with Python while keeping acceptable performance, its influence is steadily growing in the data science world.

1.7.1 Benefits and uses of Data Science and Big Data

Data science and big data are used almost everywhere in both commercial and noncommercial settings. The number of use cases is vast, and the examples we'll provide throughout this book only scratch the surface of the possibilities. Commercial companies in almost every industry use data science and big data to gain insights into their customers, processes, staff, completion, and products.

Many companies use data science to offer customers a better user experience, as well as to cross-sell, up-sell, and personalize their offerings.

A good example of this is Google AdSense, which collects data from internet users so relevant commercial messages can be matched to the person browsing the internet.

Governmental organizations are also aware of data's value. Many governmental organizations not only rely on internal data scientists to discover valuable information, but also share their data with the public. You can use this data to gain insights or build data-driven applications. Data.gov is one example, it's the home of the US Government's open data.

Nongovernmental organizations (NGOs) are also no strangers to using data. They use it to raise money and defend their causes. The World Wildlife Fund (WWF), for instance, employs data scientists to increase the effectiveness of their fundraising efforts.

Many data scientists devote part of their time to helping NGOs, because NGOs often lack the resources to collect data and employ data scientists. DataKind is one such data scientist group that devotes its time to the benefit of mankind.

The universities use data science in their research but also to enhance the study experience of their students. The rise of massive open online courses (MOOC) produces a lot of data, which allows universities to study how this type of learning can complement traditional classes.

MOOCs are an invaluable asset if you want to become a data scientist and big data professional, so definitely look at a few of the better-known ones: Coursera, Udacity, and edX. The big data and data science landscape changes quickly, and MOOCs allow you to stay up to date by following courses from top universities.

1.7.2 The Data Science Process

Following a structured approach to data science helps you to maximize your chances of success in a data science project at the lowest cost. It also makes it possible to take up a project as a team, with each team member focusing on what they do best. Take care, however: this approach may not be suitable for every type of project or be the only way to do good data science. The data science process typically consists of six steps, as you can see in the mind map in the figure.

A) Setting the Research Goal

Data science is mostly applied in the context of an organization. When the business asks you to perform a data science project, you'll first prepare a project charter. This charter contains information such as what you're going to research, how the company benefits from that, what data and resources you need, a timetable, and deliverables.

B) Retrieving Data

The second step is to collect data. You've stated in the project charter which data you need and where you can find it. In this step you ensure that you can use the data in your program, which means checking the existence of, quality, and access to the data. Data can also be delivered by third-party companies and takes many forms ranging from Excel spreadsheets to different types of databases.

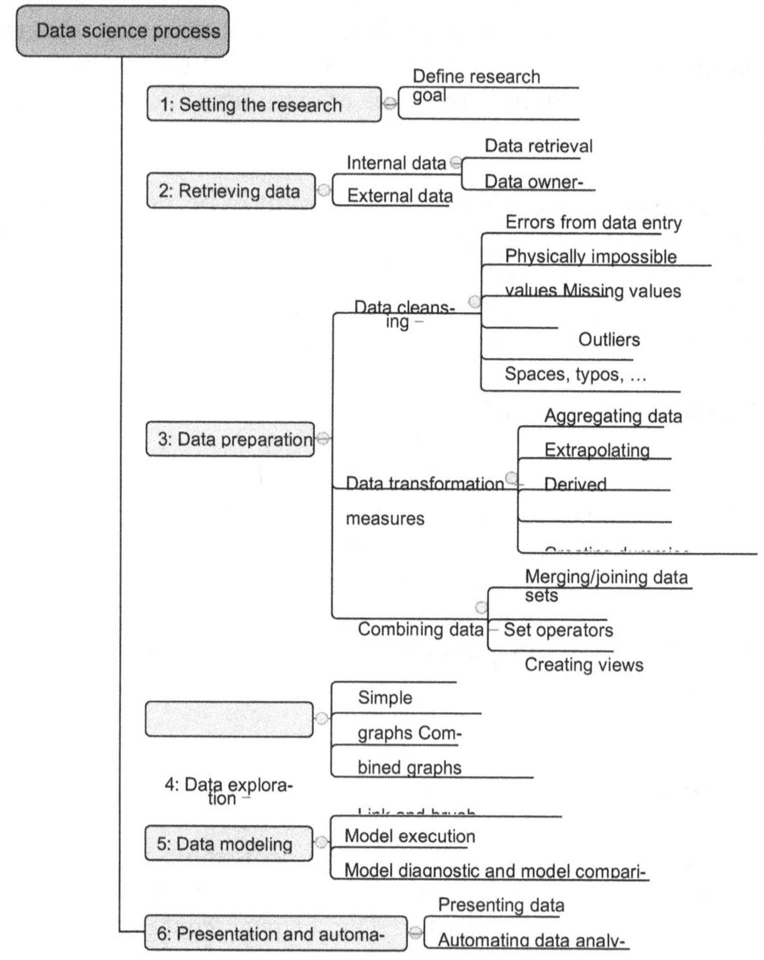

C) Data Preparation

Data collection is an error-prone process; in this phase you enhance the quality of the data and prepare it for use in subsequent steps. This phase consists of three subphases: data cleansing removes false values from a data source and inconsistencies across data sources, data integration enriches data sources by combining information from multiple data sources, and data transformation ensures that the data is in a suitable format for use in your models.

D) Data Exploration

Data exploration is concerned with building a deeper understanding of your data. You try to understand how variables interact with each other, the distribution of the data, and whether there are outliers. To achieve this, you mainly use descriptive statistics, visual techniques, and simple modeling. This step often goes by the abbreviation EDA, for Exploratory Data Analysis.

E) Data Modeling or Model Building

In this phase you use models, domain knowledge, and insights about the data you found in the previous steps to answer the research question. You select a technique from the fields of statistics, machine learning, operations research, and so on. Building a model is an iterative process that involves selecting the variables for the model, executing the model, and model diagnostics.

F) Presentation and Automation

Finally, you present the results to your business. These results can take many forms, ranging from presentations to research reports. Sometimes you'll need to automate the execution of the process because the business will want to use the insights you gained in another project or enable an operational process to use the outcome from your model.

An Iterative Process

The previous description of the data science process gives you the impression that you walk through this process in a linear way, but in reality, you often have to step back and rework certain findings. For instance, you might find outliers in the data exploration phase that point to data import errors. As part of the data science process you gain incremental insights, which may lead to new questions. To prevent rework, make sure that you scope the business question clearly and thoroughly at the start.

Who is a Data Scientist?

A Data Scientist can: - understand the background domain - design solutions that produce added value to the organization - implement the solutions efficiently - communicate the findings clearly (important!).

Data Scientist is a practitioner with sufficient expertise in software engineering, statistics/machine learning, and the application domain.

1.8 Terminologies used in Big Data Environments

The phrase Big Data has now been around for a while and we are at the stage where it is impacting more and more of us every day and it's a trend which is showing no signs of slowing down.

1. As-a-service Infrastructure: Data-as-a-service, software-as-a-service, platform-as-a-service - all refer to the idea that rather than selling data, licenses to use data, or platforms for running Big Data technology, it can be provided "as a service", rather than as a product. This reduces the upfront capital investment necessary for customers to begin putting their data, or platforms, to work for them, as the provider bears all of the costs of setting up and hosting the infrastructure. As a customer, as-a-service infrastructure can greatly reduce the initial cost and setup time of getting Big Data initiatives up and running.

2. Data Science: Data science is the professional field that deals with turning data into value such as new insights or predictive models. It brings together expertise from fields including statistics, mathematics, computer science, communication as well as domain expertise such as business knowledge. Data scientist has recently been voted the No 1 job in the U.S., based on current demand and salary and career opportunities.

3. Data Mining: Data mining is the process of discovering insights from data. In terms of Big Data, because it is so large, this is generally done by computational methods in an automated way using methods such as decision trees, clustering analysis and, most recently, machine learning. This can be thought of as using the brute mathematical power of computers to spot patterns in data which would not be visible to the human eye due to the complexity of the dataset.

4. Hadoop: Hadoop is a framework for Big Data computing which has been released into the public domain as open source software, and so can freely be used by anyone. It consists of a number of modules all tailored for a different vital step of the Big Data process – from file storage (Hadoop File System – HDFS) to database (HBase) to carrying out data operations (Hadoop MapReduce – see below). It has become so popular due to its power and flexibility that it has developed its own industry of retailers (selling tailored versions), support service providers and consultants.

5. Predictive Modelling: At its simplest, this is predicting what will happen next based on data about what has happened previously. In the Big Data age, because there is more data around than ever before, predictions are becoming more and more accurate. Predictive modelling is a core component of most Big Data initiatives, which are formulated to help us choose the course of action which will lead to the most desirable outcome. The speed of modern computers and the volume of data available means that predictions can be made based on a huge number of variables, allowing an ever-increasing number of variables to be assessed for the probability that it will lead to success.

6. MapReduce: MapReduce is a computing procedure for working with large datasets, which was devised due to difficulty of reading and analysing really Big Data using conventional computing methodologies. As its name suggest, it consists of two procedures – mapping (sorting information into the format needed for analysis – i.e. sorting a list of people according to their age) and reducing (performing an operation, such checking the age of everyone in the dataset to see who is over 21).

7. NoSQL: NoSQL refers to a database format designed to hold more than data which is simply arranged into tables, rows, and columns, as is the case in a conventional relational database. This database format has proven very popular in Big Data applications because Big

Data is often messy, unstructured and does not easily fit into traditional database frameworks.

8. Python: Python is a programming language which has become very popular in the Big Data space due to its ability to work very well with large, unstructured datasets (see Part II for the difference between structured and unstructured data). It is considered to be easier to learn for a data science beginner than other languages such as R (see also Part II) and more flexible.

9. R: R is another programming language commonly used in Big Data and can be thought of as more specialized than Python, being geared towards statistics. Its strength lies in its powerful handling of structured data. Like Python, it has an active community of users who are constantly expanding and adding to its capabilities by creating new libraries and extensions.

10. Recommendation Engine: A recommendation engine is basically an algorithm, or collection of algorithms, designed to match an entity (for example, a customer) with something they are looking for. Recommendation engines used by the likes of Netflix or Amazon heavily rely on Big Data technology to gain an overview of their customers and, using predictive modelling, match them with products to buy or content to consume. The economic incentives offered by recommendation engines has been a driving force behind a lot of commercial Big Data initiatives and developments over the last decade.

11. Real-time: Real-time means "as it happens" and in Big Data refers to a system or process which is able to give data-driven insights based on what is happening at the present moment. Recent years have seen a large push for the development of systems capable of processing and offering insights in real-time (or near-real-time), and advances in computing power as well as development of techniques such as machine learning have made it a reality in many applications today.

12. Reporting: The crucial "last step" of many Big Data initiative involves getting the right information to the people who need it to make decisions, at the right time. When this step is automated, analytics is applied to the insights themselves to ensure that they are communicated in a way that they will be understood and easy to act on. This will usually involve creating multiple reports based on the same data or insights, but each intended for a different audience (for example, in-depth technical analysis for engineers, and an overview of the impact on the bottom line for c-level executives).

13. Spark: Spark is another open-source framework like Hadoop but more recently developed and more suited to handling cutting-edge Big Data tasks involving real time analytics and machine learning. Unlike Hadoop it does not include its own filesystem, though it is designed to work with Hadoop's HDFS or a number of other options. However, for certain data related processes it is able to calculate at over 100 times the speed of Hadoop, thanks to its in-memory processing capability. This means it is becoming an increasingly popular choice for projects involving deep learning, neural networks and other compute-intensive tasks.

14. Structured Data: Structured data is simply data that can be arranged neatly into charts and tables consisting of rows, columns or multi-dimensioned matrixes. This is traditionally the way that computers have stored data, and information in this format can easily and simply be processed and mined for insights. Data gathered from machines is often a good example of structured data, where various data points - speed, temperature, rate of failure, RPM etc. - can be neatly recorded and tabulated for analysis.

15. Unstructured Data: Unstructured data is any data which cannot easily be put into conventional charts and tables. This can include video data, pictures, recorded sounds, text written in human languages and a great deal more. This data has traditionally been far harder to draw insight from using computers which were generally designed to read and analyses structured information. However, since it has become apparent that a huge amount of value can be locked away in this unstructured data, great efforts have been made to create applications which are capable of understanding unstructured data - for example visual recognition and natural language processing.

16. Visualization: Humans find it very hard to understand and draw insights from large amounts of text or numerical data - we can do it, but it takes time, and our concentration and attention is limited. For this reason, effort has been made to develop computer applications capable of rendering information in a visual form - charts and graphics which highlight the most important insights which have resulted from our Big Data projects. A subfield of reporting (see above), visualizing is now often an automated process, with visualizations customized by algorithm to be understandable to the people who need to act or take decisions based on them.

1.9 Basically Available Soft State Eventual Consistency (BASE)

Basically Available, Soft State, Eventual Consistency (BASE) is a data system design philosophy that prizes availability over consistency of operations. BASE was developed as an alternative for producing more scalable and affordable data architectures, providing more options to expanding enterprises/IT clients and simply acquiring more hardware to expand data operations.

BASE, also known as Eventual Consistency, is seen as the polar opposite of Atomicity, Consistency, Isolation, Durability (ACID), properties seen as desirable in traditional database systems such as a Relational Database Management System (RDBMS).

1.9.1 ACID versus BASE Data Stores

One hallmark of relational database systems is something known as ACID compliance. As you might have guessed, ACID is an acronym — the individual letters, meant to describe a characteristic of individual database transactions, can be expanded as described in this list:

1. **Atomicity:** The database transaction must completely succeed or completely fail. Partial success is not allowed.
2. **Consistency:** During the database transaction, the RDBMS progresses from one valid state to another. The state is never invalid.
3. **Isolation:** The client's database transaction must occur in isolation from other clients attempting to transact with the RDBMS.
4. **Durability:** The data operation that was part of the transaction must be reflected in nonvolatile storage (computer memory that can retrieve stored information even when not powered — like a hard disk) and persist after the transaction successfully completes.

Transaction failures cannot leave the data in a partially committed state.

a. Certain use cases for RDBMSs, like online transaction processing, depend on ACID-compliant transactions between the client and the RDBMS for the system to function properly. A great example of an ACID-compliant transaction is a transfer of funds from one bank account to another.

This breaks down into two database transactions, where the originating account shows a withdrawal, and the destination account shows a deposit. Obviously, these two transactions have to be tied together in order to be valid so that if either of them fail, the whole operation must fail to ensure both balances remain valid.

Hadoop itself has no concept of transactions (or even records, for that matter), so it clearly isn't an ACID-compliant system. Thinking more specifically about data storage and processing projects in the entire Hadoop ecosystem, none of them is fully ACID-compliant, either. However, they do reflect properties that you often see in NoSQL data stores, so there is some precedent to the Hadoop approach.

One key concept behind NoSQL data stores is that not every application truly needs ACID-compliant transactions. Relaxing on certain ACID properties (and moving away from the relational model) has opened up a wealth of possibilities, which have enabled some NoSQL data stores to achieve massive scalability and performance for their niche applications.

Whereas ACID defines the key characteristics required for reliable transaction processing, the NoSQL world requires different characteristics to enable flexibility and scalability. These opposing characteristics are cleverly captured in the acronym BASE:

1. **Basically Available:** The system is guaranteed to be available for querying by all users. (No isolation here.)
2. **Soft State:** The values stored in the system may change because of the eventual consistency model, as described in the next bullet.
3. **Eventually Consistent:** As data is added to the system, the system's state is gradually replicated across all nodes. For example, in Hadoop, when a file is written to the HDFS, the replicas of the data

blocks are created in different data nodes after the original data blocks have been written. For the short period before the blocks are replicated, the state of the file system isn't consistent.

The acronym BASE is a bit contrived, as most NoSQL data stores don't completely abandon all the ACID characteristics — it's not really the polar opposite concept that the name implies, in other words. Also, the Soft State and Eventually Consistent characteristics amount to the same thing, but the point is that by relaxing consistency, the system can horizontally scale (many nodes) and ensure availability.

No discussion of NoSQL would be complete without mentioning the CAP theorem, which represents the three kinds of guarantees that architects aim to provide in their systems:

4. Consistency: Similar to the C in ACID, all nodes in the system would have the same view of the data at any time.

a) **Availability:** The system always responds to requests.
b) **Partition tolerance:** The system remains online if network problems occur between system nodes.

The CAP theorem states that in distributed networked systems, architects have to choose two of these three guarantees — you can't promise your users all three. That leaves you with the three possibilities shown:

1. Systems using traditional relational technologies normally aren't partition tolerant, so they can guarantee consistency and availability. In short, if one part of these traditional relational technologies systems is offline, the whole system is offline.

2. Systems where partition tolerance and availability are of primary importance can't guarantee consistency, because updates (that destroyer of consistency) can be made on either side of the partition. The key-value stores Dynamo and CouchDB and the column-family store Cassandra are popular examples of partition tolerant/availability (PA) systems.

3. Systems where partition tolerance and consistency are of primary importance can't guarantee availability because the systems return errors until the partitioned state is resolved.

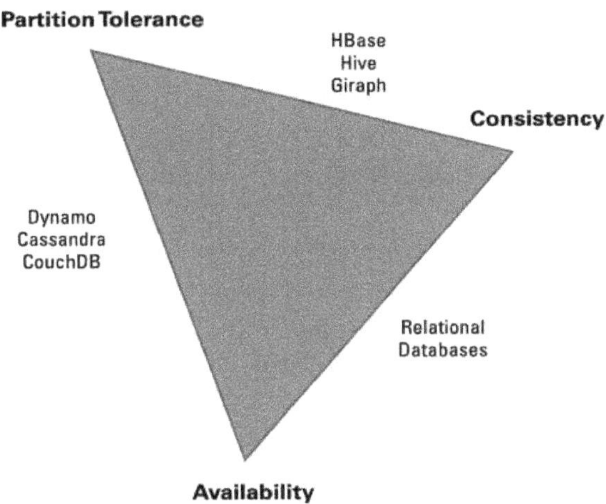

1.10 Open-Source Analytics Tools

Data, data and data. This seems to be what our world is swimming and immersing in. Why? The answer is simple: simply everything we use, such as mobile phones, and with it, all that it has, such as the social media, churn out unimaginable amounts of data.

Let us give you some perspective about data in our real world:

1. Some 1.2 trillion searches are made on Google every year;
2. Facebook users send out something like 31million+ messages and view more than 2.75 million videos every single minute;
3. For just gathering data, American companies spent over $57 billion in 2017. It is no wonder that the Gartner forecast, made in 2012, that Big Data would account for six million jobs in the US in 2015, actually outgrew the estimates by a third;
4. Five exabytes of information created from the dawn of history until 2003 is now created every two days globally!

While these figures are fascinating, why we need to be so obsessed with them is that all these gargantuan numbers could mean nothing if we did not know how to use this data. This is why the technology by which this is done, namely Data Analytics (or Big Data Analytics), is such a hot topic in the tech world today.

Like all other tools and technologies, Big Data Analytics is built on tools, frameworks and processes. Which are these? Let us look at the 5 most prominent Big Data Analytics tools to learn in 2020:

1. Microsoft HDInsight: A Spark and Hadoop cloud service, Azure HDInsight, Microsoft HDInsight comes in two categories for providing Big Data: Standard and Premium. In offering an enterprise-scale cluster that helps organizations run their big data workloads on; Microsoft HDInsight comes with the following features:

a) Its analytics capability comes an industry-leading Service Level Agreement, which makes it highly trustworthy
b) It security and monitoring are enterprise-grade
c) It is versatile, since it offers data protection of assets on-premises and its governance controls are on the cloud
d) Well suited for a number of areas, as its platform is suited for developers and scientists alike

2. Tableau Public: Another of the 5 prominent Big Data Analytics tools for 202; Tableau Public uses Tableau's USP, data visualization, for analyzing Big Data. With a limit of a humongous million rows, Tableau Public is amazingly easy to use.

It has these prominent features:

a) Its interactive data visualizations can be published on the www for free;
b) It comes with utmost ease of use, as prior programming skills are not required to use it.

3. Apache Hadoop: This Java based Big Data Analytics tool is also free. This software framework makes it easy to store huge amounts of data effectively on the cloud through clusters. Not only can Apache Hadoop run in parallel on a cluster; it can also process insancly large amounts of data across all the nodes of the cluster seamlessly.

Apache Hadoop comes with these interesting features:

a) Data processing is both fast and flexible with this tool
b) Since the nodes can communicate to each other quickly, Apache Hadoop facilitates a very effective level of performance.

4. Oracle Analytics Cloud: The way in which Oracle Analytics Cloud has been growing in the past few years has been belying the industry thought that Big Data Analytics has never been Oracle's forte. Its analytics cloud comes with these features:

a) The USP of this platform lies in the fact that its strong infrastructure enables it to bring different sources of data together, by which it offers different kinds of automation capabilities separately for different types of analytics and Big Data analysis use-cases.
b) It offers self-service Big Data Analytics, a mainstay of the analytics world.

5. Cloudera: Cloudera brings enterprise-class deployment of big Data Analytics, which it does through a combination of Apache Spark, Apache Hadoop, Apache Impala and many others. This platform aids in the collection, processing, administering, managing, discovery, modeling, and distribution of virtually unlimited data.

These are a couple of its prominent features:

a) Its distribution, as we have just seen, is vast and comprehensive
b) Better security and governance, and greater ease of use and implementation.

UNIT 2

UNDERSTANDING ANALYTICS AND BIG DATA

Living in the era of digital technology and big data has made organizations dependent on the wealth of information data can bring. You might have seen how reporting and analysis are used interchangeably, especially the manner which outsourcing companies market their services. While both areas are part of web analytics (note that analytics isn't similar to analysis), there's a vast difference between them, and it's more than just spelling.

Information is the oil of the 21st century, and analytics is the combustion engine
Peter Sondergaard, Senior Vice President, Gartner

2.1 Introduction

It's important that we differentiate the two because some organizations might be selling themselves short in one area and not reap the benefits, which web analytics can bring to the table. The first core component of web analytics, reporting, is merely organizing data into summaries. On the other hand, analysis is the process of inspecting, cleaning, transforming, and modeling these summaries (reports) with the goal of highlighting useful information.

2.2 Reporting and Analysis

Reporting: The process of organizing data into informational summaries in order to monitor how different areas of a business are performing.

Analysis: The process of exploring data and reports in order to extract meaningful insights, which can be used to better understand and improve business performance.

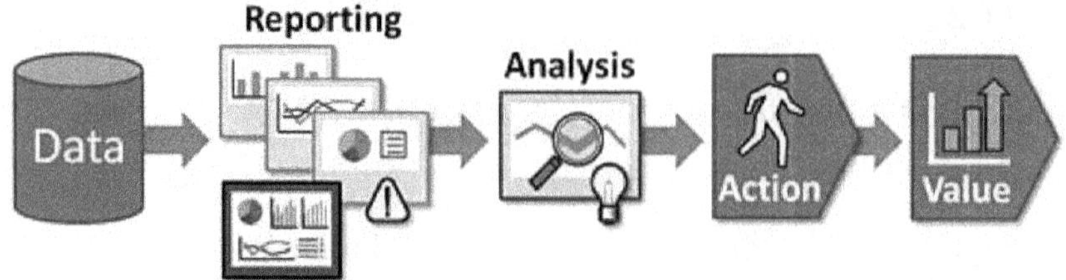

Simply put, reporting translates data into information while analysis turns information into insights. Also, reporting should enable users to ask "What?" questions about the information, whereas analysis should answer to "Why"" and "What can we do about it?"

You may have seen various people use the terms "reporting" and "analysis" as though they were interchangeable terms or almost synonyms. While both of these areas of web analytics draw upon the same collected web data, reporting and analysis are very different in terms of their purpose, tasks, outputs, delivery, and value.

Without a clear distinction of the differences, an organization may sell itself short in one area (typically analysis) and not achieve the full benefits of its web analytics investment. Although I'm primarily focusing on web analytics, companies can run into the same challenge with other analytics tools (e.g., ad serving, email, search, social, etc.).

Scope

Most companies have analytics solutions in place to derive greater value for their organizations. In other words, the ultimate goal for reporting and analysis is to increase sales and reduce costs (i.e., add value). Both reporting and analysis play roles in influencing and driving the actions which lead to greater value in organizations.

1. Purpose: Reporting translates raw data into information. Analysis transforms data and information into insights. Reporting helps companies to monitor their online business and be alerted to when data falls outside of expected ranges. Good reporting should raise questions about the business from its end users. The goal of analysis is to **answer** questions by interpreting the data at a deeper level and providing actionable recommendations. Through the process of performing analysis you may raise additional questions, but the goal is to identify answers, or at least potential answers that can be tested. In summary, reporting shows you what is happening while analysis focuses on explaining why it is happening and what you can do about it.

2. Tasks: Companies can sometimes confuse "analytics" with "analysis". For example, a firm may be focused on the general area of analytics (strategy, implementation, reporting, etc.) but not necessarily on the specific aspect of analysis. It's almost like some organizations run out of gas after the initial set-up-related activities and don't make it to the analysis stage. In addition, sometimes the lines between reporting and analysis can blur – what feels like analysis is really just another flavor of reporting.

One way to distinguish whether your organization is emphasizing reporting or analysis is by identifying the primary tasks that are being performed by your analytics team. If most of the team's time is spent on activities such as building, configuring, consolidating, organizing, formatting, and summarizing – that's reporting. Analysis focuses on different tasks such as questioning, examining, interpreting, comparing, and confirming (I've left out testing as I view optimization efforts as part of the action stage). Reporting and analysis tasks can be intertwined, but your analytics team should still evaluate where it is spending the majority of its time. In most cases, I've seen analytics teams spending most of their time on reporting tasks.

3. Outputs: When you look at reporting and analysis deliverables, on the surface they may look similar – lots of charts, graphs, trend lines, tables, stats, etc. However, there are some subtle differences. One of the main differences between reporting and analysis is the overall approach. Reporting follows a **push approach**, where reports are pushed to users who are then expected to extract meaningful insights and take appropriate actions for themselves (i.e., self-serve). I've identified three main types of reporting: canned reports, dashboards, and alerts.

a) Canned Reports

These are the out-of-the-box and custom reports that you can access within the analytics tool or which can also be delivered on a recurring basis to a group of end users. Canned reports are fairly static with fixed metrics and dimensions. In general, some canned reports are more valuable than others, and a report's value may depend on how relevant it is to an individual's role (e.g., SEO specialist vs. web producer).

b) Dashboards

These custom-made reports combine different KPIs and reports to provide a comprehensive, high-level view of business performance for specific audiences. Dashboards may include data from various data sources and are also usually fairly static.

c) Alerts

These conditional reports are triggered when data falls outside of expected ranges or some other pre-defined criteria is met. Once people are notified of what happened, they can take appropriate action as necessary.

In contrast, analysis follows a pull approach, where particular data is pulled by an analyst in order to answer specific business questions. A basic, informal analysis can occur whenever someone simply performs some kind of mental assessment of a report and makes a decision to act or not act based on the data.

In the case of analysis with actual deliverables, there are two main types: ad hoc responses and analysis presentations.

d) Ad hoc Responses

Analysts receive requests to answer a variety of business questions, which may be spurred by questions raised by the reporting. Typically, these urgent requests are time sensitive and demand a quick turnaround. The analytics team may have to juggle multiple requests at the same time. As a result, the analyses cannot go as deep or wide as the analysts may like, and the deliverable is a short and concise report, which may or may not include any specific recommendations.

e) Analysis Presentations

Some business questions are more complex in nature and require more time to perform a comprehensive, deep-dive analysis. These analysis projects result in a more formal deliverable, which includes two key sections: key findings and recommendations. The key findings section highlights the most meaningful and actionable insights gleaned from the analyses performed. The recommendations section provides guidance on what actions to take based on the analysis findings.

When you compare the two sets of reporting and analysis deliverables, the different purposes (information vs. insights) reveal the true colors of the outputs. Reporting pushes information to the organization, and analysis pulls insights from the reports and data. There may be other hybrid outputs such as annotated dashboards (analysis sprinkles on a reporting donut), which may appear to span the two areas. You should be able to determine whether a deliverable is primarily focused on reporting or analysis by its purpose (information/insights) and approach (push/pull).

Another key difference between reporting and analysis is **context**. Reporting provides no or limited context about what's happening in the data. In some cases, the end users already possess the necessary context to understand and interpret the data correctly. However, in other situations, the audience may not have the required background knowledge.

Context is critical to good analysis. In order to tell a meaningful story with the data to drive specific actions, context becomes an essential component of the storyline.

Although they both leverage various forms of data visualization in their deliverables, analysis is different from reporting because of the data points that are significant, unique, or special – and explain why they emphasizes are important to the business. Reporting may sometimes automatically highlight key changes in the data, but it's not going explain why these changes are (or aren't) important. Reporting isn't going to answer the "so what?" question on its own. If you've ever had the pleasure of being a new parent, we would compare canned reporting, dashboards, and alerts to a six-month-old infant. It cries – often loudly – when something is wrong, but it can't tell you what is exactly wrong. The parent has to scramble to figure out what's going on (hungry, dirty diaper, no pacifier, teething, tired, ear infection, new Baby Einstein DVD, etc.). Continuing the parenting metaphor, reporting is also not going to tell you how to stop the crying.

The recommendations component is a key differentiator between analysis and reporting as it provides specific guidance on what actions to take based on the key insights found in the data. Even analysis outputs such as ad hoc responses may not drive action if they fail to include recommendations. Once a recommendation has been made, **follow-up** is another potent outcome of analysis because recommendations demand decisions to be made (go/no go/explore further). Decisions precede action. Action precedes value.

4. Delivery: As mentioned, reporting is more of a push model, where people can access reports through an analytics tool, Excel spreadsheet, widget, or have them scheduled for delivery into their mailbox, mobile device, FTP site, etc. Because of the demands of having to provide periodic reports (daily, weekly, monthly, etc.) to multiple individuals and groups, automation becomes a key focus in building and delivering reports. In other words, once the report is built, how can it be automated for regular delivery? Most of the analysts who I've talked to don't like manually building and refreshing reports on a regular basis. It's a job for robots or computers, not human beings who are still paying off their student loans for 4-6 years of higher education.

On the other hand, analysis is all about human beings using their superior reasoning and analytical skills to extract key insights from the data and form actionable recommendations for their organizations. Although analysis can be "submitted" to decision makers, it is more effectively presented person-to-person. In their book "Competing on Analytics", Thomas Davenport and Jeanne Harris emphasize the importance of trust and credibility between the analyst and decision maker. Decision makers typically don't have the time or ability to perform analyses themselves. With a "close, trusting relationship" in place, the executives will frame their needs correctly, the analysts will ask the right questions, and the executives will be more likely to take action on analysis they trust.

5. Value: When it comes to comparing the different roles of reporting and analysis, it's important to understand the relationship between reporting and analysis in driving value. I like to think of the data-driven stages (data > reporting > analysis > decision > action > value) as a series of dominoes. If you remove a domino, it can be more difficult or impossible to achieve the desired value.

Path to Value Diagram

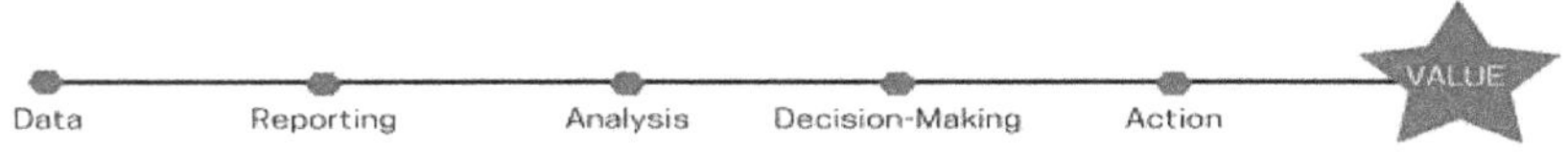

In the "Path to Value" diagram above, it all starts with having the right data that is complete and accurate. It doesn't matter how advanced your reporting or analysis is if you don't have good, reliable data. If we skip the "reporting" domino, some seasoned analysts might argue that they don't need reports to do analysis (i.e., just give me the raw files and a database). On an individual basis that might be true for some people, but it doesn't work at the organizational level if you're striving to democratize your data.

Most companies have abundant reporting but may be missing the "analysis" domino. Reporting will rarely initiate action on its own as analysis is required to help bridge the gap between data and action. Having analysis doesn't guarantee that good decisions will be made, that people will actually act on the recommendations, that the business will take the right actions, or that teams will be able to execute effectively on those right actions. However, it is a necessary step closer to action and the potential value that can be realized through successful web analytics.

	PURPOSE	TASKS	OUTPUT	DELIVERY	VALUE
REPORTING	Monitor and alert	1.Build 2.Configure 3.Consolidate 4.Organize 5.Format 6.Summarize	1.Canned reports 2.Dashboards 3.Alerts	1.Accessed via tools 2.Scheduled for delivery	1.Distills data into information for further analysis 2.Alerts company to exceptions in data
ANALYSIS	Interpret and recommend actions	1.Question 2.Examine 3.Interpret 4.Compare 5.Confirm	1.Adhoc Responses 2.Analysis Presentations (findings + recommended actions)	Prepared and presented by analyst	1.Provides deeper insights into business 2.Offers recommendations to drive action

2.3 Types of Analytics

Data analytics is the process of extracting, transforming, loading, modelling, and drawing conclusions from data to make decisions. It's the "drawing conclusions" bit that BI tools are most concerned with, as the extracting, transforming, and loading steps generally happen at the database level. There are four ways of making sense out of data once it's been formatted for reporting, and these are descriptive, diagnostic, predictive, and prescriptive analytics.

The Four Types
of
Data Analytics

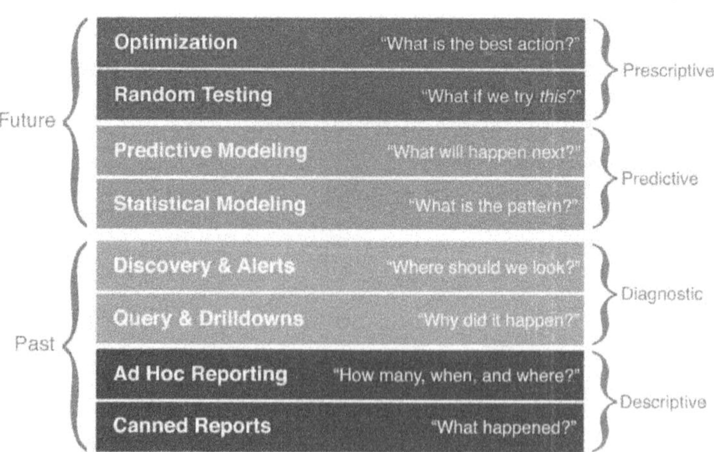

Descriptive Analytics: comprise your reporting bedrock; no BI tool is complete without it. Descriptive analytics is designed to get you basic expository information: who, what, when, where, how many? A canned report, in this instance, is a report that has been designed for you and just delivers the necessary information around a subject. A canned sales report for a magazine publisher might display the upcoming issues, the sales representatives that have sold advertising in those issues, how much they've sold, how much more they need to sell before they reach their sales quotas, and total information. An ad hoc report, by contrast, is one you've designed yourself, giving you the leverage to ask more specific questions. An ad hoc sales report at the same magazine company might include the types of advertisers each sales representative sold to, separated by industry vertical, in addition to all the other sales information included on the canned report.

Diagnostic Analytics: help you answer the question of why something happened. Queries and drill-downs enable you to request more detail related to a report, which can help explain surprising values. Referring back to our fictional magazine publisher, let's say a sales representative named Chris has sold considerably less than usual on a particular issue. A drill down showing employee work hours might reveal a three-day gap wherein Chris was out of town, explaining the discrepancy. Chris's manager trusts that he'll be able to make up for lost time but could use an alert tool to notify her if Chris's number doesn't hit a certain mark by a specified date.

Predictive Analytics: help you identify trends in relationships between variables, determine the strength of their correlation, and hypothesize causality. Statistical modelling and predictive modelling go hand in hand; the former enables the latter. Let's say that our fictional magazine publisher is considering expanding their distribution to one of two new territories, and they want some information about which will give them the highest boost in revenue. They could use statistical modelling to determine how closely revenue correlates with, for example, an area's population, median gross income, number of homeowners, etc. and with what degree of certainty. Then, using predictive modelling, they could plug in the statistics of the two territories to extrapolate a plausible revenue value for each region.

Prescriptive Analytics: is where artificial intelligence and big data come into play. Whereas statistical modelling is more about assessing correlation to prove or disprove a hypothesis, machine learning is about predicting outcomes based on numerous variables. Big data, staggeringly large sets of information often reflecting crowd behavior and sourced from outside the company in question, is essential to machine learning because it is complex enough to refine the artificial intelligence's decisions over time. AI can give probable answers to what-if questions such as, "What if we run an article about reclaimed furniture in our next issue?" and suggest courses of action, like to write about reclaimed patio furniture in particular, which will be trending next month for the target demographic.

2.4 Data Analysis

Data Analysis is a process of collecting, transforming, cleaning, and modeling data with the goal of discovering the required information. The results so obtained are communicated, suggesting conclusions, and supporting decision-making. Data visualization is at times used to portray the data for the ease of discovering the useful patterns in the data. The terms Data Modeling and Data Analysis mean the same.

Data Analysis Process consists of the following phases that are iterative in nature:

1. Data Requirements Specification
2. Data Collection
3. Data Processing
4. Data Cleaning
5. Data Analysis
6. Communication

1. Data Requirements Specification

The data required for analysis is based on a question or an experiment. Based on the requirements of those directing the analysis, the data necessary as inputs to the analysis is identified (e.g., Population of people). Specific variables regarding a population (e.g., Age and Income) may be specified and obtained. Data may be numerical or categorical.

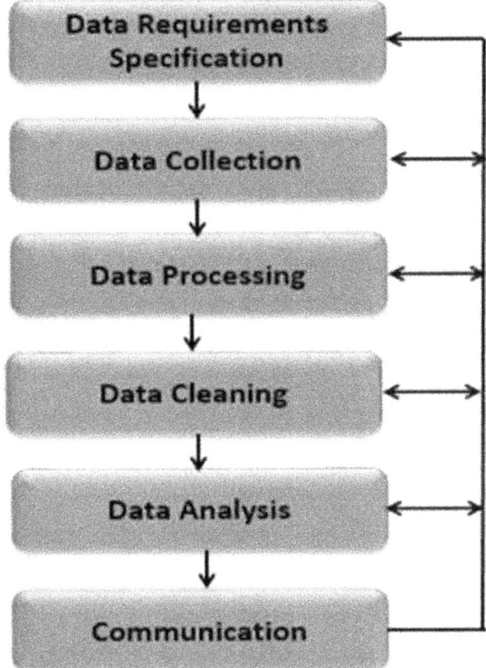

2. Data Collection

Data Collection is the process of gathering information on targeted variables identified as data requirements. The emphasis is on ensuring accurate and honest collection of data. Data Collection ensures that data gathered is accurate such that the related decisions are valid. Data Collection provides both a baseline to measure and a target to improve.

Data is collected from various sources ranging from organizational databases to the information in web pages. The data thus obtained, may not be structured and may contain irrelevant information. Hence, the collected data is required to be subjected to Data Processing and Data Cleaning.

3. Data Processing

The data that is collected must be processed or organized for analysis. This includes structuring the data as required for the relevant

Analysis Tools. For example, the data might have to be placed into rows and columns in a table within a Spreadsheet or Statistical Application. A Data Model might have to be created.

4. Data Cleaning

The processed and organized data may be incomplete, contain duplicates, or contain errors. Data Cleaning is the process of preventing and correcting these errors. There are several types of Data Cleaning that depend on the type of data. For example, while cleaning the financial data, certain totals might be compared against reliable published numbers or defined thresholds. Likewise, quantitative data methods can be used for outlier detection that would be subsequently excluded in analysis.

5. Data Analysis

Data that is processed, organized and cleaned would be ready for the analysis. Various data analysis techniques are available to understand, interpret, and derive conclusions based on the requirements. Data Visualization may also be used to examine the data in graphical format, to obtain additional insight regarding the messages within the data.

Statistical Data Models such as Correlation, Regression Analysis can be used to identify the relations among the data variables. These models that are descriptive of the data are helpful in simplifying analysis and communicate results.

The process might require additional Data Cleaning or additional Data Collection, and hence these activities are iterative in nature.

6. Communication

The results of the data analysis are to be reported in a format as required by the users to support their decisions and further action. The feedback from the users might result in additional analysis.

The data analysts can choose data visualization techniques, such as tables and charts, which help in communicating the message clearly and efficiently to the users. The analysis tools provide facility to highlight the required information with color codes and formatting in tables and charts.

2.5 Developing an Analytic Team

Data Analyst

1. The main responsibility of a data analyst is to take business data, such as sales figures, logistics and market figures), analyze it and use the information to help managers make better business decisions.
2. While managers usually make decisions based on what they think is the right decision for the business, they usually need to back their decisions with facts, and that is where data analysts come in.
3. Usually, data analysts are required to present all the data they have collected and analyzed. The presentation must be in a simple format, which the average person can understand.
4. After presentation of the information, the analyst will recommend a number of options for the managers to consider.

A) Skills Needed by a Data Analyst

1. Data analysts need a myriad of skills to do their job. Some of the most important skills include; business analysis, data analysis, data architecture, social/behavioral analysis, mathematics and statistics, and data interpretation and visualization skills.
2. To succeed in this industry, data scientists need five core competencies; Programming, Statistics, Machine Learning, Data Visualization and Data Munging.
3. From these core competencies of a data scientist, you can see that there are two main backgrounds where data scientists can come from. These are; computer science/programming and mathematics/statistics.
4. Anyone who has an undergraduate degree in these fields can join a graduate school to study and become a data analyst. Other fields, such as actuarial science, are also related to this field.

B) How to Structure a High Performance Analytics Team

Analytics have become paramount to a company's success and achieving a competitive edge over the competition. Let me state for the record, there is no perfect way to structure an analytics team. There are multiple ways teams are structured these days, and additionally if you search on Google, you'll find a handful of different structures that are being used. What I will highlight in this article, is what I believe to be the best way to structure a team.

The most important thing a business can do, is asking why they need analytics. Also, having a good sense of the different types of analytics techniques will help you frame who you need on the team.

Analytics is defined as, the systematic computational analysis of data or statistics.

Analytics is the umbrella for — data visualization (dashboards), EDA, machine learning, AI, etc.

Core Analytics / Data Mining Methods

1. Descriptive — what has happened and is happening?
2. Prescriptive — find the best course of action for a given problem
3. Exploratory — what nuggets exist in my data?
4. Predictive — what will happen in the future

Who makes up the core of the Analytics team?

- Data Analysts
- Data Engineers
- Data Scientists

C) What Do These Roles Do?

a) Data Analyst

1. Generalist who can fit into many roles and teams to help others make data driven decisions

2. Data Analyst deliver value by taking data, using it to answer questions, and communicate the results to help make business decisions

b) Data Scientist

1. Specialist that applies expertise in statistics and building machine learning models to make predictions and answer key business questions
2. Has all the skills a data analyst does, but will have more depth and expertise in those skills
3. Discover hidden insights in data by leveraging supervised and unsupervised machine learning models

c) Data Engineer

1. Build and optimize the systems that allow data scientist and analysts to perform their work. Ensures data is properly received, transformed, stored, and made accessible to other users
2. Leans heavier in software development skill set

d) Analytics Manager

Who should manage the Analytics Team? An Analytics Manager (also known as Head of Analytics, or Data Analytics Manager) If the team is only 2 people, this won't make much sense. However, if you have a team of 3+ you need a manager.

The Analytics Manager's main responsibilities are:

1. Managing the data warehousing and ETL solutions
2. Prioritizing projects based on the best ROI (the manager must have strong domain knowledge and a deep understanding of the businesses core objectives)
3. Shielding Data Analysts from being bombarded with reporting and visualization requests
4. Ensuring that the team has all of the tools they need to complete their projects
5. Influencing the business to be a data driven culture

6. Encouraging self service analytics
7. Providing direction on predictive and prescriptive analytics projects
8. Mentoring and providing continuous educational opportunities for the team to stay on top of their roles

e) Director of Analytics

In some instances, depending on the size of the organization you can have a structure as follows.

Director of Analytics > Analytics Manager and Data Science Manager

1. The Director of Analytics manages the Analytics and Data Science manager(s)
2. The Analytics Manager would oversee the Data Engineers and Data Analysts, focusing on exploratory and descriptive analytics.
3. The Data Science Manager would oversee the Data Scientists, focusing on predictive and prescriptive analytics.

2.6 Mapping the Ideal Analyst Workload

What is the most effective mix of responsibilities for each analyst position under perfect conditions? Our first step was to diagram the ideal division of work for our analytics team:

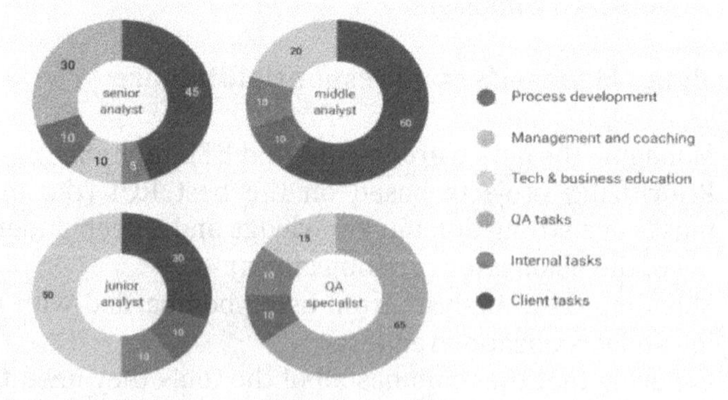

So, for example, in a company, senior analysts spend:

- 45% of their time on tasks from clients;
- 30% of their time on management and coaching;
- 10% of their time on tech and business education;
- 10% of their time on process development;
- 5% of their time on internal tasks.

This ideal task distribution, as we later learned, was far from reality. That gap resulted from eight key challenges faced by our team.

2.7 How to Build an Analytics Team for Impact in an Organization

They say that wisdom comes with experience, and we'd have to agree with that. Having spent the past two years building an analytics team with the primary aim of having impact in the business, it's only now that we feel we can say something about how to do that.

One of the reasons why it has taken me some time to form a point of view is that we have experimented with a few different models and structures in order to find out which ones work most effectively. Another reason is that no single individual has the answer, and it has taken time for our model to develop through a consultative approach with key members of the team and important stakeholders in the business.

That said, the model around which an analytics team should operate within a business or organization has now formed more solidly in my mind. It has six steps which form a 'lifecycle' around business decision-making. These six steps inform how the team should operate, what skills are required, how the team should be structured and what types of profiles and skills should be present on the team. I realize that many of those who read this article will not necessarily have access to the resources required to fully comply with this model, often because the organization they serve is too small to justify it, but nevertheless I believe the overall picture is still of interest.

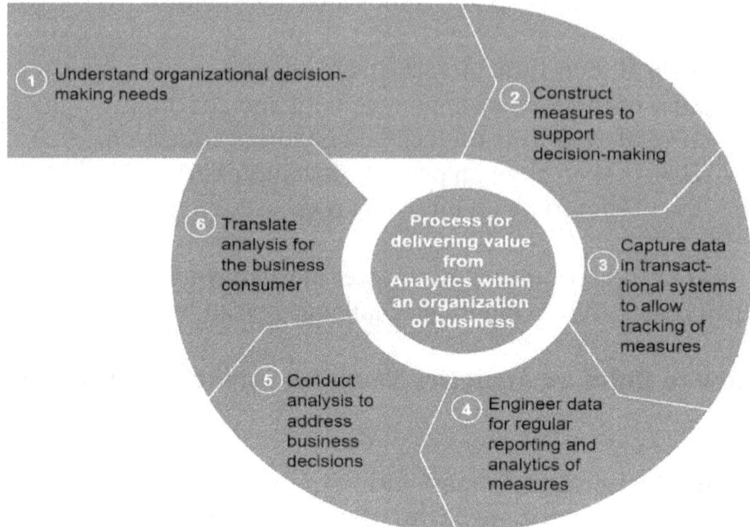

Step 1: Understand the decision-making needs of the business

Why? One of the common reasons why analytics teams do not function optimally is a lack of understanding of the decision-making that occurs in the business they serve. If an analytics team is overly staffed with technically or academically minded individuals, this 'conceptual gap' is highly likely to affect the potential for impact of the team, because analytics will often be driven by the personal interests of those on the team and not against the requirements of the key internal clients.

How? At least one of the senior members of the analytics team should be closely connected to the decision-making organs of the business, be it the CFO, CHRO or the other committees or groups which are tasked with making the critical business decisions. Regular forums should be set up where the key priorities of the business are communicated as well as feedback on where analytic intelligence is lacking. This will allow the formation of an analytics agenda, and the building of data structures and tools which will best serve the future needs of key internal clients. The individual responsible for this should ideally be sourced from the business itself, be analytically and strategically minded (though not necessarily technically skilled), and have a passion and drive to develop analytics and analytic capabilities within the business.

Step 2: Construct measures to support business decision-making

Why? My regular readers will likely be tired of hearing this from me, but analytics success depends on effective measurement. Many analytics teams struggle today because they are not accessing accurate measurement data. Upon understanding the decision-making needs of the business, the first question to be asked should be 'What would we need to measure to understand this?'. Measurement can be a fiendishly difficult problem. Determining the appropriate measure is a delicate balance of mathematical and statistical principles set alongside considerations of data systems and data capture processes as well as human behaviors. It's often a compromise, but it needs to have strong expertise and judgment to get it right.

How? Determining measurement approaches to address a particular business problem requires participation from many skill sets on the analytics team. A measurement expert is an absolute necessity. For example, this could be a psychometric an if it is a people and skills problem, or a marketing metrics expert if it is a sales or marketing problem. Alongside the measurement expert, input is needed from a data expert, usually an engineer who understands the transactional systems and the flow of data, an analytics professional such as a data scientist who understands how to work with data in conducting analytics, and finally the individual from Step 1 who will be able to properly explain and translate the decision making needs of the business to the technical experts.

Step 3: Capture data in transactional systems to allow tracking of measures

Why? If the measures that arise from step two are new, then more often than not it will require the entry of a new type of data at an atomic level within the organization. This will require implementation as a systems level, as well as an understanding of the rules and logic required and the adjustments needed to human processes to ensure the data is captured accurately.

How? The data engineer is a foundational role in any analytics team. They will act as the key liaison with the system administrators and experts, and they need to have an important say on how the fields and entry rules are constructed within transactional systems to allow for accurate and reliable data flows. This is not their only critical role (see next step).

Step 4: Engineer data for regular reporting and analytics of measures

Why? The process needed to translate transactional business data into measures that are useful for analysis and decision making can be laborious. Some careful thought around this can make a huge difference to the efficiency and reliability of an analytics operation. Can the transactional data be pre-processed on a regular basis (hourly, daily, weekly, monthly) to create tables or views that are aggregated at a level allow for more rapid analysis and insight? How should these views be designed? What demographics or cuts should be available?

How? A capable data engineer can work wonders in both understanding the needs for pre-processing of data and in actually creating and designing the required aggregated data sources.

Step 5: Conduct analysis to address business questions

Why? This part is obvious.

How? This deserves a fuller treatment which I will focus on in a future article. Clear lines needs to be drawn between

- Regular standardized reporting, which requires data science, data engineering, visualization, UX and software development skills in data automation and provision. Ideally, almost no team time should be spent on delivering regular reporting manually. External vendor products may help plug gaps here, but my experience is that no vendor tool satisfies the entire plethora of needs here. The best teams will design this for themselves.
- Ad hoc analytics, which require business intelligence professionals who understand the data systems of the organization and can use them to satisfy the specific, non-standard questions which come in from business customers.
- Advanced analytics, which requires deep knowledge of advanced statistical methods and fluency with advanced data science tools to allow data to be analyzed and processed using these advanced methods,

Step 6: Translate analysis for the business consumer

Why? One of the main reasons why analytics does not have impact in business and organization is that the results are not well understood, and often conclusions are drawn which are clearly wrong due to the lack of effective communication of results. To have impact in an organization, an analytics team needs to be able to draw on skills that facilitate clear translation of the results in a way that can be understood by business leaders, many of whom may not have the knowledge or skills to translate for themselves. This is particularly important when advanced methods of analysis are being employed.

How? The translator is a critical role in an effective analytics team. Translators have an understanding of organizational strategy and decision-making, strong general problem solving skills, a passion for and an interest in analytics and a client-service mindset. Analytics translators are currently the most difficult profiles to find because the role is so new and not well understood. In my experience, the most effective and able translators are sourced from the business itself. Translators provide overall leadership and direction and work with the technical skillsets (data science, measurement, engineering, visualization and design) to find the best possible solution to the client's needs. Translators maintain long term client relationships within the business to allow readjustment of the analytics approach as needs change.

2.8 Understanding Text Analytics

Text Analysis is about parsing texts in order to extract machine-readable facts from them. The purpose of Text Analysis is to create structured data out of free text content. The process can be thought of as slicing and dicing heaps of unstructured, heterogeneous documents into easy-to-manage and interpret data pieces. Text Analysis is close to other terms like Text Mining, Text Analytics and Information Extraction

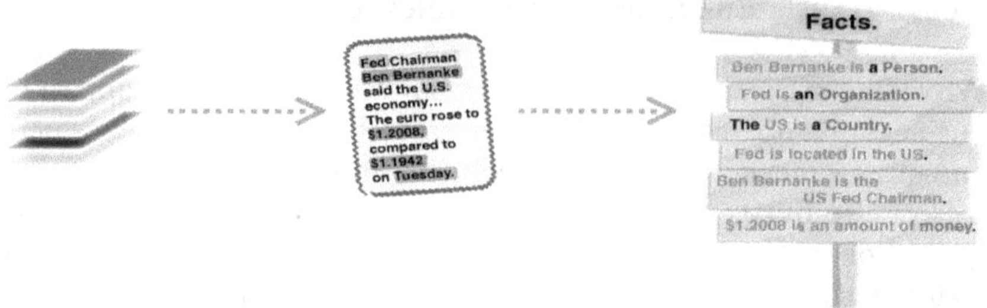
Fed Chairman
Ben Bernanke
said the U.S.
economy...
The euro rose to
$1.2008,
compared to
$1.1942
on Tuesday.
Facts.
Ben Bernanke is a Person.
Fed is an Organization.
The US is a Country.
Fed is located in the US.
Ben Bernanke is the US Fed Chairman.
$1.2008 is an amount of money.

Text data analytics uses several techniques to achieve that. These techniques are derived from multiple disciplines, such as Natural Language Processing (NLP), data mining, knowledge discovery, statistics, computational linguistics, and so on, along with many other complimentary tools.

One should note that text analytics do not only mean a keyword search, although it is indeed sometimes a part of it. There is a very fundamental difference. In text analytics, the primary focus is in extracting relevant information without actually knowing what we may get, whereas in searches we use keywords to retrieve relevant information, but the result is always known or predictable. Text analytics works on the principle of information discovery. So, the analytics uses the search as a technique or means to categorize or classify documents and to get a gist of the content.

The Techniques

Natural Language Processing (NLP), in combination with statistics, is commonly used to extract information out of unstructured data. NLP is a complex and widely researched field developed over two decades to derive meaningful information from text. It historically has been used by computation linguistics to identify meaningful sentences by using a grammatical structure and parts of speech. Text analytics uses this technique to identify the nature of data. The NLP analyses are performed on several levels, such as:

1. Morphological Level Analysis: Analysis at this level deals with the structure of the word and its formation. Here, the focus is on the individual component of the meaningful word, referred to as a morpheme. For example, the three morphemes of the word, say, "unavoidable," is un/avoid/able (prefix/stem/suffix), where each has its significant meaning. Thus, to increase recall, text analytics matches the morphological variants of documents or unstructured texts.

2. Lexical Analysis: Lexical analysis is the study of words according to some dictionary or thesaurus. An individual unit of lexical meaning is termed as a lexeme. For example, when analyzing documents, the words sales, sale, purchase, purchases, payment, and the like may add up to the idea of the occurrence of some form of transactions that we may be interested to find out further.

3. Syntactic Analysis: Syntactic analysis focuses on the grammatical aspect of the text. Here, the focus extends from individual words to phrase, clause, and sentence. The main process is to parse the sentences and group them into phrases and clauses. For example, if we analyze a sentence: Mother looked after the child; the syntactic analyses would tag the phrases found in the sentence with parts-of-speech tags.

4. Semantic Analysis: Semantics analysis determines the meaningfulness of a sentence by examining the word order and sentence structure while disambiguating the sentence according to the syntax preserved in the sentence and paragraph in the document. This increases the query precision, thus increasing the recall in the process, as well.

5. Discourse Level Analysis: Here, the analysis goes beyond a single sentence. The focus is on the structure and meaning of the words and sentences by making connections among many of them. This level is where Anaphora Resolution (AR) is achieved by picking entity references by an anaphor. Note that AR is the problem of resolving the meaning of a sentence with reference to antecedent or precedent items in the discourse. It is a challenge to optimize and is an active area of research in computational linguistics.

Analytical Approach and Tools to Analyze Data

Companies that are not leveraging data analytic tools and techniques are falling apart. Since data analytics tools capture in products that automatically glean and analyze data, deliver information and predictions, you can improve prediction accuracy and refine the models. Here we discuss the top 10 Data Analytics Tools for achieving success.

Goals of Performing Data Analysis

You can analyze data. Extract actionable and commercially relevant information to boost performance. Several extraordinary analytical tools are available, that is the free and open source so that you can leverage it to enhance your business and develop skills.

2.9 Data Analytics Tools

Here is the list of top Analytics tools for data analysis that are available for free (for personal use), easy to use (no coding required), well-documented (you can Google your way through if you get stuck) and have powerful capabilities (more than excel). These data analysis tools will help you manage and interpret data in a better and more effective way. Here, we have explored the top 10 Data Analytics tools in Big Data.

1. Tableau Public

Tableau, one of the top 10 Data Analytics tools, is a simple and intuitive and tool which offers intriguing insights through data visualization. Tableau Public's million row limit, which is easy to use fares better than most of the other players in the data analytics market.

With Tableau's visuals, you can investigate a hypothesis, explore the data, and cross-check your insights.

Uses of Tableau Public

1. You can publish interactive data visualizations to the web for free.
2. No programming skills required.
3. Visualizations published to Tableau Public can be embedded into blogs and web pages and be shared through email or social media. The shared content can be made available s for downloads.

Limitations of Tableau Public

1. All data is public and offers very little scope for restricted access
2. Data size limitation
3. Cannot be connected to
4. The only way to read is via OData sources, is Excel or txt.

2. OpenRefine

Formerly known as GoogleRefine, the data cleaning software that helps you clean up data for analysis. It operates on a row of data which have cells under columns, quite similar to relational database tables.

Uses of OpenRefine

1. Cleaning messy data
2. Transformation of data
3. Parsing data from websites
4. Adding data to the dataset by fetching it from web services. For instance, OpenRefine could be used for geocoding addresses to geographic coordinates.

Limitations of OpenRefine

1. Open Refine is unsuitable for large datasets.
2. Refine does not work very well with big data.

3. KNIME

KNIME, ranked among the top Data Analytics tools helps you to manipulate, analyze, and model data through visual programming. It is used to integrate various components for data mining and machine learning via its modular data pipelining concept.

Uses of KNIME

1. Rather than writing blocks of code, you just have to drop and drag connection points between activities.
2. This data analysis tool supports programming languages.

3. In fact, analysis tools like these can be extended to run chemistry data, text mining, python, and R.

Limitation of KNIME

Poor data visualization

4. RapidMiner

RapidMiner provides machine learning procedures and data mining including data visualization, processing, statistical modeling, deployment, evaluation, and predictive analytics. RapidMiner, counted among the top 10 Data Analytics tools, is written in the Java and fast gaining acceptance.

Uses of RapidMiner

It provides an integrated environment for business analytics, predictive analysis, text mining, data mining, and machine learning. Along with commercial and business applications, RapidMiner is also used for application development, rapid prototyping, training, education, and research.

Limitations of RapidMiner

1. RapidMiner has size constraints with respect to the number of rows.
2. For RapidMiner, you need more hardware resources than ODM and SAS.

5. Google Fusion Tables

When talking about Data Analytics tools for free, here comes a much cooler, larger, and needier version of Google Spreadsheets. An incredible tool for data analysis, mapping, and large dataset visualization, Google Fusion Tables can be added to business analytics tools list. Ranked among the top 10 Data Analytics tools, Google Fusion Tables is fast gaining popularity.

Uses of Google Fusion Tables

1. Visualize bigger table data online:
2. Filter and summarize across hundreds of thousands of rows.
3. Combine tables with other data on the web:
   - You can merge two or three tables to generate a single visualization that includes sets of data. With Google Fusion Tables, you can combine public data with your own for a better visualization.

Limitations of Google Fusion Tables

1. Only the first 100,000 rows of data in a table are included in query results or mapped.
2. The total size of the data sent in one API call cannot be more than 1MB.

6. NodeXL

NodeXL is a free and open-source network analysis and visualization software. Ranked among the top 10 Data Analytics tools, it is one of the best statistical tools for data analysis which includes advanced network metrics, access to social media network data importers, and automation.

Uses of NodeXL

1. Data Import
2. Graph Visualization
3. Graph Analysis
4. Data Representation

NodeXL integrates into Microsoft Excel 2007, 2010, 2013, and 2016. It opens as a workbook with a variety of worksheets containing the elements of a graph structure like nodes and edges. It can import various graph formats like adjacency matrices, Pajek .net, UCINet.dl, GraphML, and edge lists.

Limitations of NodeXL

1. Multiple seeding terms are required for a particular prob-

lem.

2. Need to run the data extractions at slightly different times.

7. Wolfram Alpha

Wolfram Alpha, one of the top 10 Data Analytics tools is a computational knowledge engine or answering engine founded by Stephen Wolfram. With Wolfram Alpha, you get answers to factual queries directly by computing the answer from externally sourced 'curated data' instead of providing a list of documents or web pages.

Uses of Wolfram Alpha

1. Is an add-on for Apple's Siri
2. Provides detailed responses to technical searches and solves calculus problems.
3. Helps business users with information charts and graphs, and helps in creating topic overviews, commodity information, and high-level pricing history.

Limitations of Wolfram Alpha

1. Wolfram Alpha can only deal with the publicly known number and facts, not with viewpoints.
2. It limits the computation time for each query.

8. Google Search Operators

It is a powerful resource that helps you filter Google results instantly to get the most relevant and useful information.

Uses of Google Search Operators

1. Fast filtering of Google results.
2. Google's powerful data analysis tool can help discover new information or market research.

9. Solver

The Solver Add-in is a Microsoft Office Excel add-in program that is available when you install Microsoft Excel or Office. Ranked among the best-known Data Analytic tools is a linear programming and optimization tool in excel. This allows you to set constraints. It is an advanced optimization tool that helps in quick problem-solving.

Uses of Solver

The final values found by Solver are a solution to interrelation and decision. It uses a variety of methods, from nonlinear optimization and linear programming to evolutionary and genetic algorithms, to find solutions. It is one of the top 10 Data Analytic tools in use.

Limitations of Solver

1. Poor scaling is one of the areas where Excel Solver lacks.
2. It can affect solution time and quality.
3. Solver affects the intrinsic solvability of your model.

10. Dataiku DSS

Ranked among the top 10 Data Analytic tools, Dataiku is a collaborative data science software platform that helps the team build, prototype, explore, and deliver their own data products more efficiently.

Uses of Dataiku DSS

It provides an interactive visual interface where they can build, click, and point or use languages like SQL. This data analytics tool lets you draft data preparation and modulization in seconds. Helps you coordinate development and operations by handling workflow automation, creating predictive web services, model health on a daily basis, and monitoring data.

Limitation of Dataiku DSS

1. Limited visualization capabilities
2. UI hurdles: Reloading of code/datasets
3. Inability to easily compile entire code into a single document/notebook
4. Still, need to integrate with SPARK

Comparison of Top Data Analytics Tools

Data Analysis Tool	Platform	Ratings	Verdict	Price
Zoho Analytics	Cloud, Windows, Linux, Mac, Android, iOS	5 stars	User friendly data visualization tool. Value for money.	Free Plan. Cloud: Starts at $22/month (Basic); On-premise: Starts at $150/month.
Tableau Public	Windows, Mac, Web-based, Android, iOS	5 stars	Nice tool available for free with good features and functionalities.	Tableau Public: Free Tableau Creator: $70 per user per month.
Rapid Miner	Cross-platform	5 stars	System is easy to use. Powerful GUI. Five products to choose from.	Free: 10,000 data rows. Small: $2500 per user/year. Medium: $5000 per user/year. Large: $10000 per user/year.
KNIME	Windows, Mac, Linux.	4 stars	Works with Microsoft Azure and AWS. Easy to learn software.	KNIME Analytics platform: Free. KNIME Server: Starts at $8500
Orange	Windows, Mac, Linux.	4 stars	User-friendly graphical interface	Free

Data Analysis Tool	Platform	Ratings	Verdict	Price
orange				
OpenRefine OpenRefine	Windows, Mac, Linux.	4 stars	Desktop application Multiple rows selection with filters.	Free

2.10 Widely Used Data Analytics Techniques

Here are some of the top Data Analytic tools and techniques that can be used for better performance:

1. Visual Analytics

There are different ways to analyze the data. One of the simplest ways to do is to create a graph or visual and look at it to spot patterns. This is an integrated method that combines data analysis with human interaction and data visualization.

2. Business Experiments

Experimental design, AB testing, and business experiments are all techniques for testing the validity of something. It is trying out something in one part of the organization and comparing it with another.

3. Regression Analysis

It is a statistical tool for investigating the relationship between variables. For instance, the cause and effect relationship between product demand and price.

4. Correlation Analysis

A statistical technique that allows you to determine whether there is a relationship between two separate variables and how strong that relationship may be. It is best to use when you know or suspect that there is a relationship between two variables and wish to test the assumption.

5. Time Series Analysis

It is the data that is collected at uniformly spaced time intervals. You can use it when you want to assess changes over time or predict future events on the basis of what happened in the past.

Data Analysis Methods

There are two methods of data analysis:

1. Qualitative Analysis
2. Quantitative Analysis

Qualitative Analysis: Qualitative Analysis is done through interviews and observations.

Quantitative Analysis: Quantitative Analysis is done through surveys and experiments.

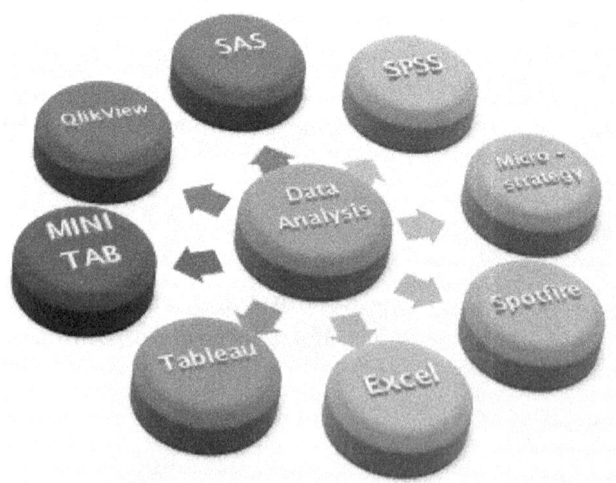

Data Analytics Process

1. Data collection
2. Working on data quality
3. Building the model
4. Training model
5. Running the model with full data

Difference Between Data Analysis, Data Mining & Data Modeling

Data analysis is done with the purpose of finding answers to specific questions. Data analytics techniques are similar to business analytics and business intelligence.

Data Mining is about finding the different patterns in data. For this, various mathematical and computational algorithms are applied to data and new data will get generated.

Data Modeling is about how companies organize or manage the data. Here, various methodologies and techniques are applied to data. Data analysis is required for data modeling.

UNIT 3

UNDERSTANDING MAPREDUCE FUNDAMENTALS AND HBASE

Hadoop is a Big Data framework designed and deployed by Apache Foundation. It is an open-source software utility that works in the network of computers in parallel to find solutions to Big Data and process it using the MapReduce algorithm. Google released a paper on MapReduce technology in December 2004. This became the genesis of the Hadoop Processing Model. So, MapReduce is a programming model that allows us to perform parallel and distributed processing on huge data sets.

Hiding within those mounds of data is knowledge that could change the life of a patient, or change the world
Atul Butte, Stanford

3.1 Introduction

MapReduce is a programming model for writing applications that can process Big Data in parallel on multiple nodes. MapReduce provides analytical capabilities for analyzing huge volumes of complex data. MapReduce, which is one of the core building blocks of processing in Hadoop framework. Big Data can be termed as that colossal load of data that can be hardly processed using the traditional data processing units. A better example of Big Data would be the currently trending Social Media sites like Facebook, Instagram, WhatsApp and YouTube.

Traditional Enterprise Systems normally have a centralized server to store and process data. The following illustration depicts a schematic view of a traditional enterprise system. Traditional model is certainly not suitable to process huge volumes of scalable data and cannot be accommodated by standard database servers. Moreover, the centralized system creates too much of a bottleneck while processing multiple files simultaneously.

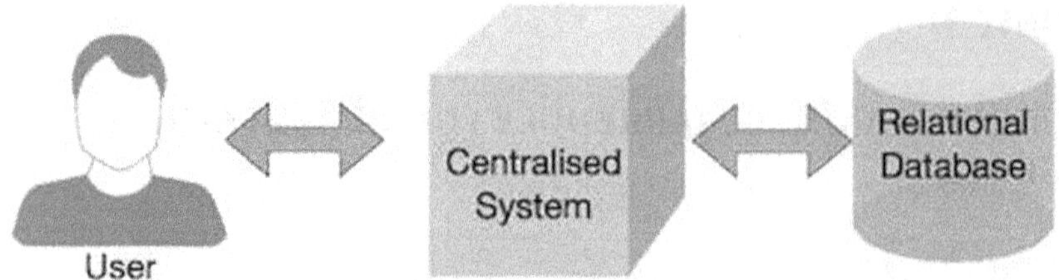

Google solved this bottleneck issue using an algorithm called MapReduce. MapReduce divides a task into small parts and assigns them to many computers. Later, the results are collected at one place and integrated to form the result dataset.

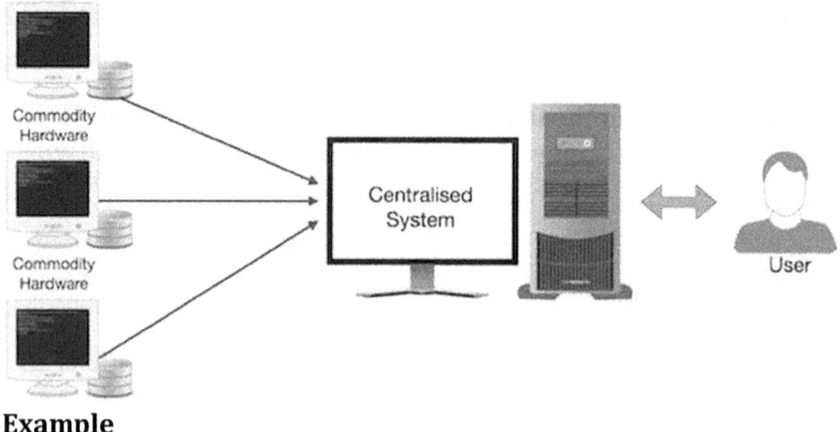

Example

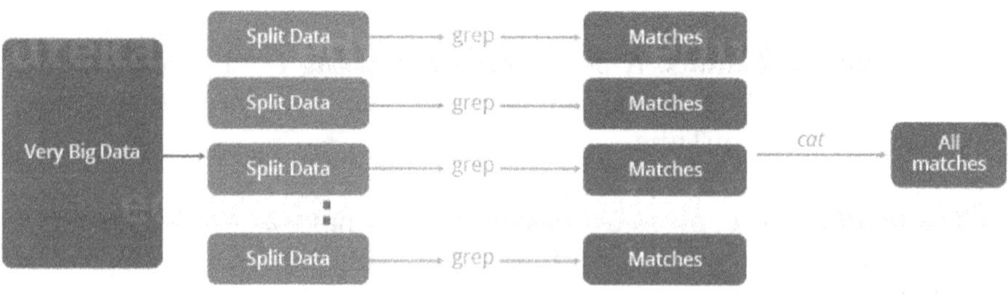

Let us understand, when the MapReduce framework was not there, how parallel and distributed processing used to happen in a traditional way. So, let us take an example where I have a weather log containing the daily average temperature of the years from 2000 to

2015. Here, I want to calculate the day having the highest temperature in each year.

So, just like in the traditional way, I will split the data into smaller parts or blocks and store them in different machines. Then, I will find the highest temperature in each part stored in the corresponding machine. At last, I will combine the results received from each of the machines to have the final output. Let us look at the challenges associated with this traditional approach:

1. **Critical path problem:** It is the amount of time taken to finish the job without delaying the next milestone or actual completion date. So, if, any of the machines delay the job, the whole work gets delayed.
2. **Reliability problem:** What if, any of the machines which are working with a part of data fails? The management of this failover becomes a challenge.
3. **Equal split issue:** How will I divide the data into smaller chunks so that each machine gets even part of data to work with. In other words, how to equally divide the data such that no individual machine is overloaded or underutilized.
4. **The single split may fail:** If any of the machines fail to provide the output, I will not be able to calculate the result. So, there should be a mechanism to ensure this fault tolerance capability of the system.
5. **Aggregation of the result:** There should be a mechanism to aggregate the result generated by each of the machines to produce the final output.

These are the issues which have to be taken care individually while performing parallel processing of huge data sets when using traditional approaches.

To overcome these issues, we have the MapReduce framework which allows us to perform such parallel computations without bothering about the issues like reliability, fault tolerance etc. Therefore, MapReduce gives you the flexibility to write code logic without caring about the design issues of the system.

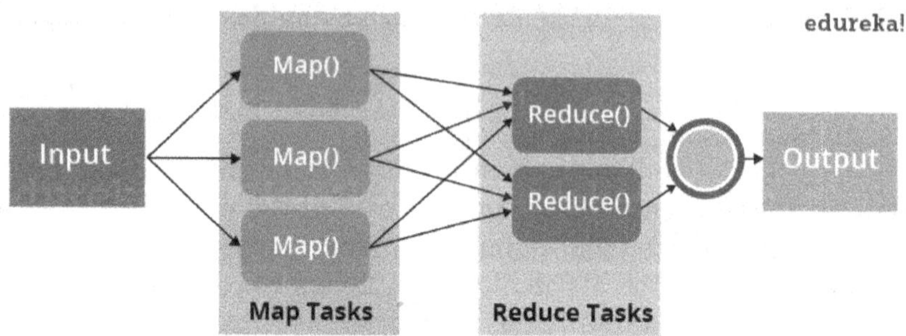

3.2 How MapReduce Works?

The MapReduce algorithm contains two important tasks, namely Map and Reduce.

1. The Map task takes a set of data and converts it into another set of data, where individual elements are broken down into tuples (key-value pairs).
2. The Reduce task takes the output from the Map as an input and combines those data tuples (key-value pairs) into a smaller set of tuples.

The reduce task is always performed after the map job.

Let us now take a close look at each of the phases and try to understand their significance.

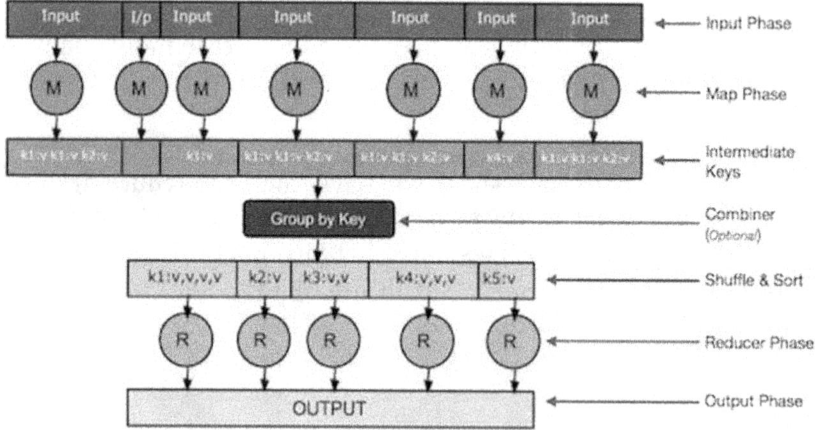

1. **Input Phase** – Here we have a Record Reader that translates each record in an input file and sends the parsed data to the mapper in the form of key-value pairs.
2. **Map** – Map is a user-defined function, which takes a series of key-value pairs and processes each one of them to generate zero or more key-value pairs.
3. **Intermediate Keys** – They key-value pairs generated by the mapper are known as intermediate keys.
4. **Combiner** – A combiner is a type of local Reducer that groups similar data from the map phase into identifiable sets. It takes the intermediate keys from the mapper as input and applies a user-defined code to aggregate the values in a small scope of one mapper. It is not a part of the main MapReduce algorithm; it is optional.
5. **Shuffle and Sort** – The Reducer task starts with the Shuffle and Sort step. It downloads the grouped key-value pairs onto the local machine, where the Reducer is running. The individual key-value pairs are sorted by key into a larger data list. The data list groups the equivalent keys together so that their values can be iterated easily in the Reducer task.
6. **Reducer** – The Reducer takes the grouped key-value paired data as input and runs a Reducer function on each one of them. Here, the data can be aggregated, filtered, and combined in a number of ways, and it requires a wide range of processing. Once the execution is over, it gives zero or more key-value pairs to the final step.
7. **Output Phase** – In the output phase, we have an output formatter that translates the final key-value pairs from the Reducer function and writes them onto a file using a record writer.

3.2.1 The Algorithm

1. Generally, MapReduce paradigm is based on sending the computer to where the data resides!
2. MapReduce program executes in three stages, namely map stage, shuffle stage, and reduce stage.

    Map stage – The map or mapper's job is to process the input data. Generally, the input data is in the form of file or directory and is stored in the Hadoop file system (HDFS). The input file is passed to the mapper function line by line. The mapper processes the data and creates several small chunks of data.

Reduce stage – This stage is the combination of the **Shuffle** stage and the **Reduce** stage. The Reducer's job is to process the data that comes from the mapper. After processing, it produces a new set of output, which will be stored in the HDFS.

3. During a MapReduce job, Hadoop sends the Map and Reduce tasks to the appropriate servers in the cluster.
4. The framework manages all the details of data-passing such as issuing tasks, verifying task completion, and copying data around the cluster between the nodes.
5. Most of the computing takes place on nodes with data on local disks that reduces the network traffic.
6. After completion of the given tasks, the cluster collects and reduces the data to form an appropriate result, and sends it back to the Hadoop server.

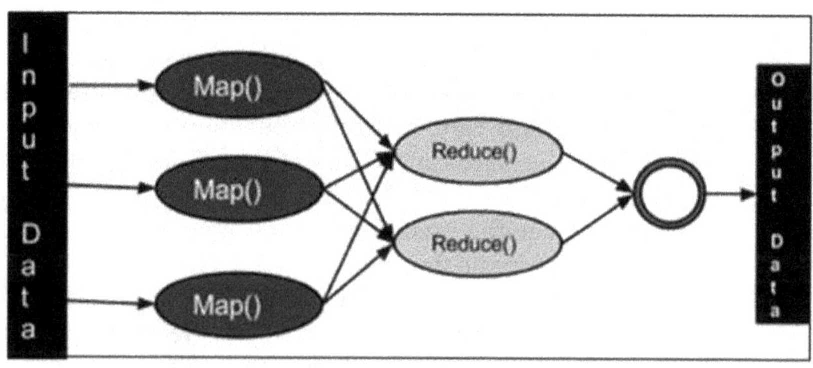

3.2.2 Map Reduce Tasks

The MapReduce algorithm contains two important tasks, namely Map and Reduce.

1. The map task is done by means of Mapper Class
2. The reduce task is done by means of Reducer Class

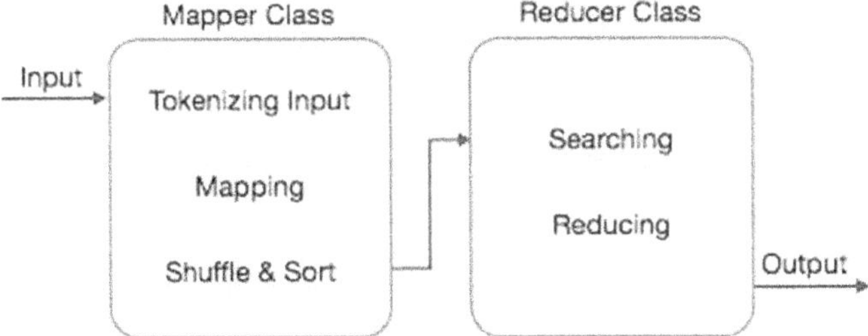

Mapper class takes the input, tokenizes it, maps and sorts it. The output of Mapper class is used as input by Reducer class, which in turn searches matching pairs and reduces them.

MapReduce implements various mathematical algorithms to divide a task into small parts and assign them to multiple systems. In technical terms, MapReduce algorithm helps in sending the Map & Reduce tasks to appropriate servers in a cluster.

These mathematical algorithms may include the following,

1. Sorting
2. Searching
3. Indexing
4. TF-IDF

1. Sorting

Sorting is one of the basic MapReduce algorithms to process and analyze data. MapReduce implements sorting algorithm to automatically sort the output key-value pairs from the mapper by their keys.

1. Sorting methods are implemented in the mapper class itself.
2. In the Shuffle and Sort phase, after tokenizing the values in the mapper class, the **Context** class (user-defined class) collects the matching valued keys as a collection.
3. To collect similar key-value pairs (intermediate keys), the Mapper class takes the help of **RawComparator** class to sort the key-value pairs.
4. The set of intermediate key-value pairs for a given Reducer is automatically sorted by Hadoop to form key-values (K2,

{V2, V2, ...}) before they are presented to the Reducer.

2. Searching

Searching plays an important role in MapReduce algorithm. It helps in the combiner phase (optional) and in the Reducer phase. Let us try to understand how Searching works with the help of an example.

Example

The following example shows how MapReduce employs Searching algorithm to find out the details of the employee who draws the highest salary in a given employee dataset.

Let us assume we have employee data in four different files – A, B, C, and D. Let us also assume there are duplicate employee records in all four files because of importing the employee data from all database tables repeatedly. See the following illustration.

name, salary	**name, salary**	**name, salary**	**name, salary**
satish, 26000	gopal, 50000	satish, 26000	satish, 26000
Krishna, 25000	Krishna, 25000	kiran, 45000	Krishna, 25000
Satishk, 15000	Satishk, 15000	Satishk, 15000	manisha, 45000
Raju, 10000	Raju, 10000	Raju, 10000	Raju, 10000

a) The Map phase processes each input file and provides the employee data in key-value pairs (<k, v> : <emp name, salary>). See the following illustration.

<satish, 26000>	<gopal, 50000>	<satish, 26000>	<satish, 26000>
<Krishna, 25000>	<Krishna, 25000>	<kiran, 45000>	<Krishna, 25000>
<Satishk, 15000>	<Satishk, 15000>	<Satishk, 15000>	<manisha, 45000>
<Raju, 10000>	<Raju, 10000>	<Raju, 10000>	<Raju, 10000>

b) The combiner phase (searching technique) will accept the input from the Map phase as a key-value pair with employee name and salary. Using searching technique, the combiner will check all the employee salary to find the highest salaried employee in each file. See the following snippet.

```
<k: employee name, v: salary>
Max= the salary of an first employee. Treated as max salary
if(v(second employee).salary > Max){
  Max = v(salary);
}
else{
  Continue checking;
}
```

The expected result is as follows

<satish, 26000>	<gopal, 50000>	<kiran, 45000>	<manisha, 45000>

c) Reducer phase – Form each file, you will find the highest salaried employee. To avoid redundancy, check all the <k, v> pairs and eliminate duplicate entries, if any. The same algorithm is used in between the four <k, v> pairs, which are coming from four input files. The final output should be as follows –
<gopal, 50000>

3. Indexing

Normally indexing is used to point to a particular data and its address. It performs batch indexing on the input files for a particular Mapper.

The indexing technique that is normally used in MapReduce is known as **inverted index.** Search engines like Google and Bing use inverted indexing technique. Let us try to understand how Indexing works with the help of a simple example.

Example

The following text is the input for inverted indexing. Here T[0], T[1], and t[2] are the file names and their content are in double quotes.
T[0] = "it is what it is"
T[1] = "what is it"
T[2] = "it is a banana"

After applying the Indexing algorithm, we get the following output –
"a": {2}
"banana": {2}
"is": {0, 1, 2}
"it": {0, 1, 2}
"what": {0, 1}
Here "a": {2} implies the term "a" appears in the T[2] file. Similarly, "is": {0, 1, 2} implies the term "is" appears in the files T[0], T[1], and T[2].

4. TF-IDF

TF-IDF is a text processing algorithm which is short for Term Frequency – Inverse Document Frequency. It is one of the common web analysis algorithms. Here, the term 'frequency' refers to the number of times a term appears in a document.

Term Frequency (TF)

It measures how frequently a particular term occurs in a document. It is calculated by the number of times a word appears in a document divided by the total number of words in that document.

TF(the) = (Number of times term the 'the' appears in a document) / (Total number of terms in the document)
Inverse Document Frequency (IDF)

It measures the importance of a term. It is calculated by the number of documents in the text database divided by the number of documents where a specific term appears.

While computing TF, all the terms are considered equally important.

That means, TF counts the term frequency for normal words like "is", "a", "what", etc. Thus we need to know the frequent terms while scaling up the rare ones, by computing the following,

IDF(the) = log_e(Total number of documents / Number of documents with term 'the' in it).

The algorithm is explained below with the help of a small example.

Example

Consider a document containing 1000 words, wherein the word **hive** appears 50 times. The TF for **hive** is then (50 / 1000) = 0.05.

Now, assume we have 10 million documents and the word **hive** appears in 1000 of these. Then, the IDF is calculated as log(10,000,000 / 1,000) = 4.

The TF-IDF weight is the product of these quantities – 0.05 × 4 = 0.20.

Let us try to understand the two tasks Map &f Reduce with the help of a small diagram

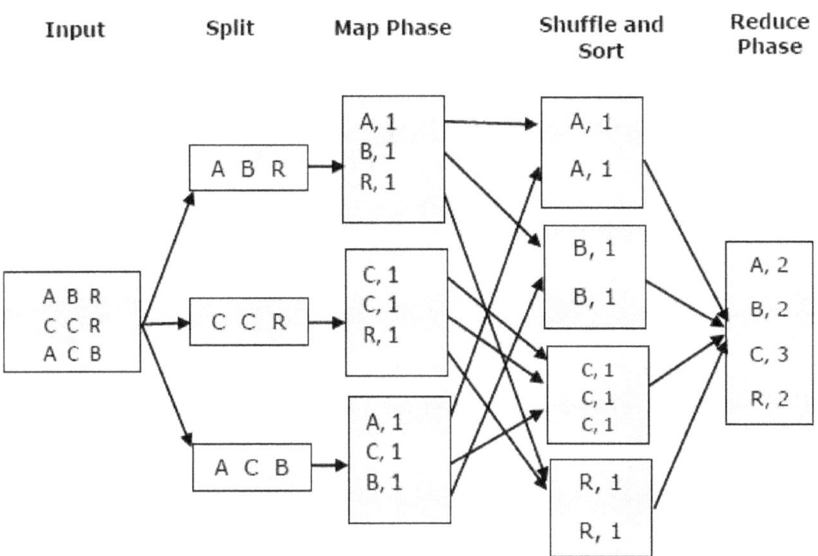

Let us understand, how a MapReduce works by taking an example where I have a text file called example.txt whose contents are as follows:

Dear, Bear, River, Car, Car, River, Deer, Car and Bear

Now, suppose, we have to perform a word count on the sample.txt using MapReduce. So, we will be finding the unique words and the number of occurrences of those unique words.

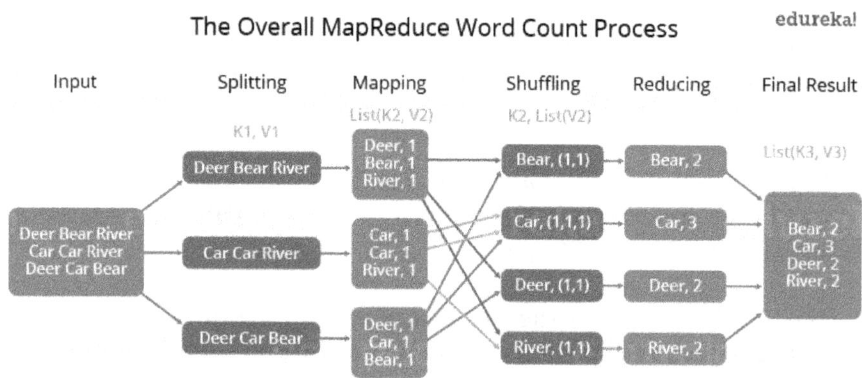

1. First, we divide the input into three splits as shown in the figure. This will distribute the work among all the map nodes.
2. Then, we tokenize the words in each of the mappers and give a hardcoded value (1) to each of the tokens or words. The rationale behind giving a hardcoded value equal to 1 is that every word, in itself, will occur once.
3. Now, a list of key-value pair will be created where the key is nothing but the individual words and value is one. So, for the first line (Dear Bear River) we have 3 key-value pairs – Dear, 1; Bear, 1; River, 1. The mapping process remains the same on all the nodes.
4. After the mapper phase, a partition process takes place where sorting and shuffling happen so that all the tuples with the same key are sent to the corresponding reducer.
5. So, after the sorting and shuffling phase, each reducer will have a unique key and a list of values corresponding to that very key. For example, Bear, [1,1]; Car, [1,1,1].., etc.

6. Now, each Reducer counts the values which are present in that list of values. As shown in the figure, reducer gets a list of values which is [1,1] for the key Bear. Then, it counts the number of ones in the very list and gives the final output as – Bear, 2.

Finally, all the output key/value pairs are then collected and written in the output file.

3.2.3 Advantages of MapReduce

The two biggest advantages of MapReduce are,

Parallel Processing

In MapReduce, we are dividing the job among multiple nodes and each node works with a part of the job simultaneously. So, MapReduce is based on Divide and Conquer paradigm which helps us to process the data using different machines. As the data is processed by multiple machines instead of a single machine in parallel, the time taken to process the data gets reduced by a tremendous amount as shown in the figure below.

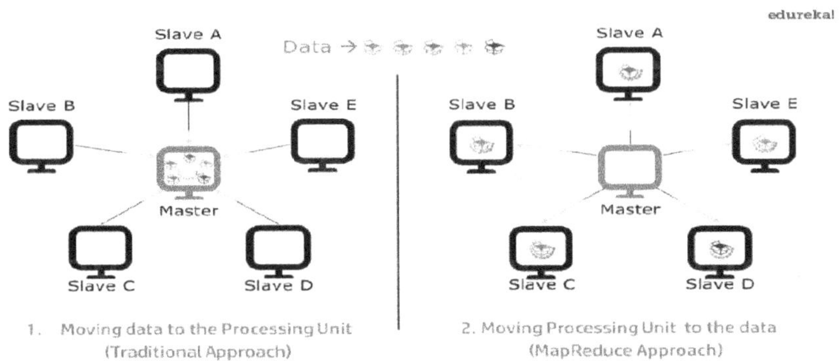

Data Locality

Instead of moving data to the processing unit, we are moving the processing unit to the data in the MapReduce Framework. In the traditional system, we used to bring data to the processing unit and process it. But, as the data grew and became very huge, bringing this huge amount of data to the processing unit posed the following issues:

1. Moving huge data to processing is costly and deteriorates the network performance.
2. Processing takes time as the data is processed by a single unit which becomes the bottleneck.
3. The master node can get over-burdened and may fail.

Now, MapReduce allows us to overcome the above issues by bringing the processing unit to the data. So, as you scan see in the above image that the data is distributed among multiple nodes where each node processes the part of the data residing on it. This allows us to have the following advantages:

1. It is very cost-effective to move processing unit to the data.
2. The processing time is reduced as all the nodes are working with their part of the data in parallel.
3. Every node gets a part of the data to process and therefore, there is no chance of a node getting overburdened.

3.3 Introduction to HBase

Since 1970, RDBMS is the solution for data storage and maintenance related problems. After the advent of big data, companies realized the benefit of processing big data and started opting for solutions like Hadoop.

Hadoop uses distributed file system for storing big data, and MapReduce to process it. Hadoop excels in storing and processing of huge data of various formats such as arbitrary, semi-, or even unstructured.

Limitations of Hadoop

Hadoop can perform only batch processing, and data will be accessed only in a sequential manner. That means one has to search the entire dataset even for the simplest of jobs.

A huge dataset when processed results in another huge data set, which should also be processed sequentially. At this point, a new solution is needed to access any point of data in a single unit of time (random access).

Hadoop Random Access Databases

Applications such as HBase, Cassandra, couchDB, Dynamo, and MongoDB are some of the databases that store huge amounts of data and access the data in a random manner.

What is HBASE?

HBase is an open-source, column-oriented distributed database system in a Hadoop environment. Initially, it was Google Big Table, afterward; it was re-named as HBase and is primarily written in Java. Apache HBase is needed for real-time Big Data applications.

HBase can store massive amounts of data from terabytes to petabytes. The table present in HBase consists of billions of rows having millions of columns. HBase is built for low latency operations, which is having some specific features compared to traditional relational models.

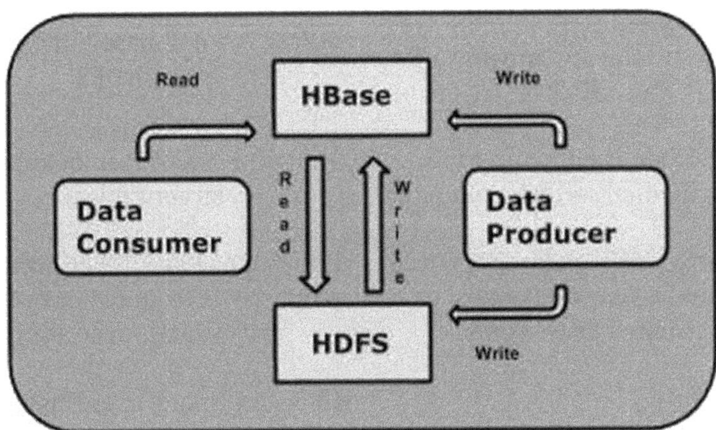

HBase Unique Features

1. HBase is built for low latency operations
2. HBase is used extensively for random read and write operations

3. HBase stores a large amount of data in terms of tables
4. Provides linear and modular scalability over cluster environment
5. Strictly consistent to read and write operations
6. Automatic and configurable sharing of tables
7. Automatic failover supports between Region Servers
8. Convenient base classes for backing Hadoop MapReduce jobs in HBase tables
9. Easy to use Java API for client access
10. Block cache and Bloom Filters for real-time queries
11. Query predicate pushes down via server-side filters.

One can store the data in HDFS either directly or through HBase. Data consumer reads/accesses the data in HDFS randomly using HBase. HBase sits on top of the Hadoop File System and provides read and write access.

Comparison of HBase and HDFS

HDFS	HBase
HDFS is a distributed file system suitable for storing large files.	HBase is a database built on top of the HDFS.
HDFS does not support fast individual record lookups.	HBase provides fast lookups for larger tables.
It provides high latency batch processing; no concept of batch processing.	It provides low latency access to single rows from billions of records (Random access).
It provides only sequential access of data.	HBase internally uses Hash tables and provides random access, and it stores the data in indexed HDFS files for faster lookups.

3.3.1 Storage Mechanism in HBase

HBase is a **column-oriented database** and the tables in it are sorted by row. The table schema defines only column families, which are the key value pairs. A table have multiple column families and each column family can have any number of columns. Subsequent column values are stored contiguously on the disk. Each cell value of the table has a timestamp. In short, in an HBase:

- Table is a collection of rows.
- Row is a collection of column families.
- Column family is a collection of columns.
- Column is a collection of key value pairs.

Given below is an example schema of table in HBase

Row -id	**Column Family**			**Column Family**			**Column Family**			**Column Family**		
	col 1	**col 2**	**col 3**	**col 1**	**col 2**	**col 3**	**col 1**	**col 2**	**col 3**	**col 1**	**col 2**	**col 3**
1												
2												
3												

Column Oriented and Row Oriented: Column-oriented databases are those that store data tables as sections of columns of data, rather than as rows of data. Shortly, they will have column families.

Row-Oriented Database	**Column-Oriented Database**
It is suitable for Online Transaction Process (OLTP).	It is suitable for Online Analytical Processing (OLAP).
Such databases are designed for small number of rows and columns.	Column-oriented databases are designed for huge tables.

The following image shows column families in a column-oriented database:

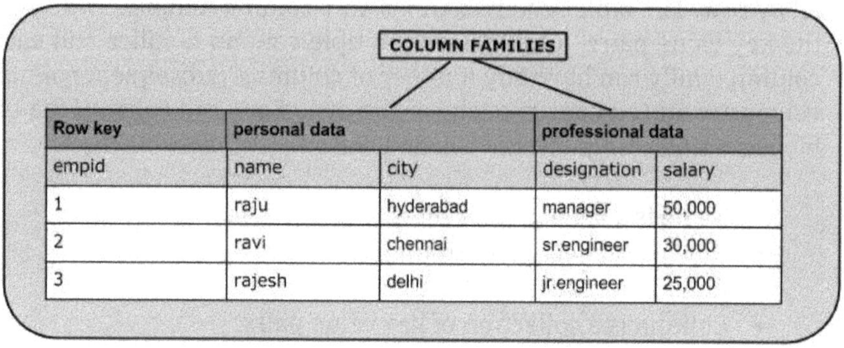

COLUMN FAMILIES

Row key	personal data		professional data	
empid	name	city	designation	salary
1	raju	hyderabad	manager	50,000
2	ravi	chennai	sr.engineer	30,000
3	rajesh	delhi	jr.engineer	25,000

Where to Use HBase

1. Apache HBase is used to have random, real-time read/write access to Big Data.
2. It hosts very large tables on top of clusters of commodity hardware.
3. Apache HBase is a non-relational database modeled after Google's Bigtable. Bigtable acts up on Google File System, likewise Apache HBase works on top of Hadoop and HDFS.

Applications of HBase

1. It is used whenever there is a need to write heavy applications.
2. HBase is used whenever we need to provide fast random access to available data.
3. Companies such as Facebook, Twitter, Yahoo, and Adobe use HBase internally.

HBase History

Year	Event
Nov 2006	Google released the paper on BigTable.

Feb 2007	Initial HBase prototype was created as a Hadoop contribution.
Oct 2007	The first usable HBase along with Hadoop 0.15.0 was released.
Jan 2008	HBase became the sub project of Hadoop.
Oct 2008	HBase 0.18.1 was released.
Jan 2009	HBase 0.19.0 was released.
Sept 2009	HBase 0.20.0 was released.
May 2010	HBase became Apache top-level project.

3.3.2 HBase – Architecture

In HBase, tables are split into regions and are served by the region servers. Regions are vertically divided by column families into "Stores". Stores are saved as files in HDFS. Shown below is the architecture of HBase.

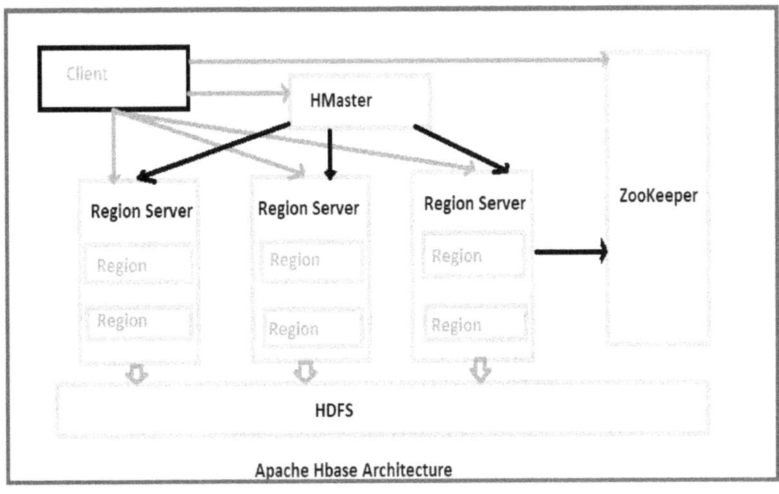

Apache Hbase Architecture

HBase architecture consists mainly the following components

1. HMaster
2. HRegionserver
3. HRegions
4. Zookeeper
5. HDFS

1. HMaster

HMaster is the implementation of a Master server in HBase architecture. It acts as a monitoring agent to monitor all Region Server instances present in the cluster and acts as an interface for all the metadata changes. In a distributed cluster environment, Master runs on NameNode. Master runs several background threads.

The following are important roles performed by HMaster in HBase.

1. Plays a vital role in terms of performance and maintaining nodes in the cluster.
2. HMaster provides admin performance and distributes services to different region servers.
3. HMaster assigns regions to region servers.
4. HMaster has the features like controlling load balancing and failover to handle the load over nodes present in the cluster.
5. When a client wants to change any schema and to change any Metadata operations, HMaster takes responsibility for these operations.

Some of the methods exposed by HMaster Interface are primarily Metadata oriented methods.

- Table (createTable, removeTable, enable, disable)
- ColumnFamily (add Column, modify Column)
- Region (move, assign)

The client communicates in a bi-directional way with both HMaster and ZooKeeper. For read and write operations, it directly contacts with HRegion servers. HMaster assigns regions to region servers and in turn, check the health status of region servers.

In entire architecture, we have multiple region servers. Hlog present in region servers which are going to store all the log files.

2. HBase Regions Servers

When Region Server receives writes and read requests from the client, it assigns the request to a specific region, where the actual column family resides. However, the client can directly contact with HRegion servers, there is no need of HMaster mandatory permission to the client regarding communication with HRegion servers. The client requires HMaster help when operations related to metadata and schema changes are required. HRegionServer is the Region Server implementation. It is responsible for serving and managing regions or data that is present in a distributed cluster. The region servers run on Data Nodes present in the Hadoop cluster. HMaster can get into contact with multiple HRegion servers and performs the following functions.

- Hosting and managing regions
- Splitting regions automatically
- Handling read and writes requests
- Communicating with the client directly

3. HBase Regions

HRegions are the basic building elements of HBase cluster that consists of the distribution of tables and are comprised of Column families. It contains multiple stores, one for each column family. It consists of mainly two components, which are Memstore and Hfile.

4. ZooKeeper

In HBase, ZooKeeper is a centralized monitoring server which maintains configuration information and provides distributed synchronization. Distributed synchronization is to access the distributed applications running across the cluster with the responsibility of providing coordination services between nodes. If the client wants to communicate with regions, the server's client has to approach ZooKeeper first. It is an open-source project, and it provides so many important services.

Services provided by ZooKeeper:

1. Maintains Configuration information
2. Provides distributed synchronization
3. Client Communication establishment with region servers
4. Provides ephemeral nodes for which represent different region servers
5. Master servers usability of ephemeral nodes for discovering available servers in the cluster
6. To track server failure and network partitions

Master and HBase slave nodes (region servers) registered themselves with ZooKeeper. The client needs access to ZK(zookeeper) quorum configuration to connect with master and region servers. During a failure of nodes that present in HBase cluster, ZKquoram will trigger error messages, and it starts to repair the failed nodes.

Interacting with the Hadoop Ecosystem

Let's see where HBase sits in the Hadoop ecosystem. In the Hadoop ecosystem, HBase provides a persistent, structured, schema-based data store. The following figure illustrates the Hadoop ecosystem:

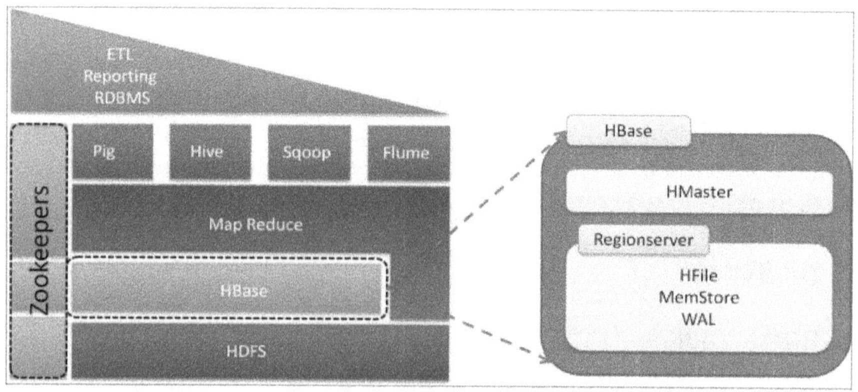

HBase can work as a separate entity on the local file system (which is not really effective as no distribution is provided) as well as in coordination with Hadoop as a separate but connected entity. As we know, Hadoop provides two services, a distributed files system (HDFS) for storage and a MapReduce framework for processing in a parallel mode. When there was a need to store structured data (data in the form of tables, rows and columns), which most of the programmers are already familiar with, the programmers were finding it difficult to process the data that was stored on HDFS as an unstructured flat file format. This led to the evolution of HBase, which provided a way to store data in a structural way.

Consider that we have got a CSV file stored on HDFS and we need to query from it. We would need to write a Java code for this, which wouldn't be a good option. It would be better if we could specify the data key and fetch the data from that file. So, what we can do here is create a schema or table with the same structure of CSV file to store the data of the CSV file in the HBase table and query using HBase APIs, or HBase shell using key.

HBase in Operations-Programming with HBase Installation

HBase is the open-source implementation of Google's Big Table, with slight modifications. HBase was created in 2007 and was initially a part of contributions to Hadoop which later became a top-level Apache project. It is a distributed column-oriented key value database built on top of the Hadoop file system and is horizontally scalable which means that we can add the new nodes to Hbase when data grows. But, how is the data Read or Written to the tables? This is the topic of discussion in this blog. Readers are requested to go through few blogs which might help get a clear understanding of HBase.

3.3.3 Hbase Major Components

Two major components which play a vital role in data read and write are, HFile and META Table.

HFile

It is the basic level HBase architecture where the tables exist in physical form. It is important to understand this component since *Read* and Write take place here. The key features of HFile are:

- Row key is primary identifier.
- Keys are stored in lexicographical order.

- According to this order, data is stored and split across the nodes.
- HFile is allocated to 1 region
- HFiles store the rows in sorted by KeyValues on disk.
- When the MemStore accumulates data more than its limit, the entire sorted set is written to a new HFile in HDFS.
- HBase uses multiple HFiles per column family, containing the actual cells, or KeyValue instances.
- The highest sequence number is stored as a meta field in each HFile, to a better state where it has ended previously and where to continue next.
- HFile contains a multi-layered index which allows HBase to search the data without having to read the whole file.
- HDFS replicates the WAL and HFile blocks.
- HFile block replication happens automatically.
- IO in HBase happens at HFile block level which is 64KB by default.
- One HFile can contain only one column family. What if data grows in a particular HFile?
- Different HFile is created with same column family and writing data is continued.
- No two column families can exist in single HFile.

META Table

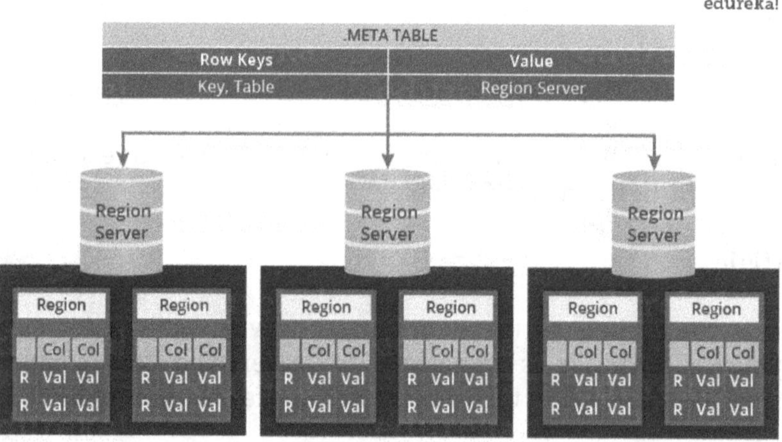

The META table is a special HBase catalog table. It maintains a list of all the Regions Servers in the HBase storage system, as you can see in the above image. Looking at the figure you can see, **.META** file maintains the table in form of keys and values. Key represents the start key of the region and its id whereas the value contains the path of the Region Server.

HBase Read and Write Data

The Read and Write operations from Client into Hfile can be shown in below diagram.

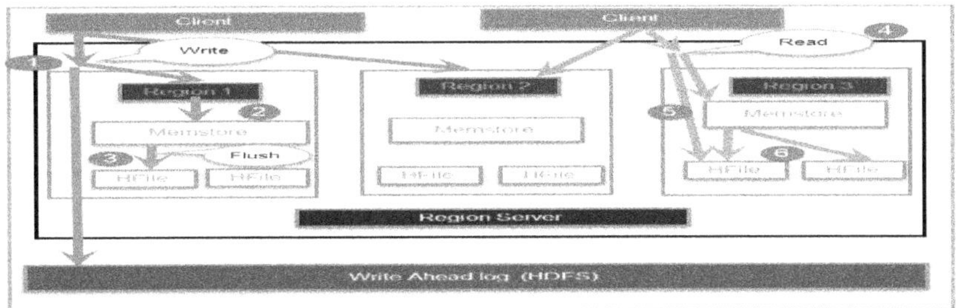

3.3.4 Components of Region Server

This below image shows the components of a Region Server. Now, we will discuss them separately.

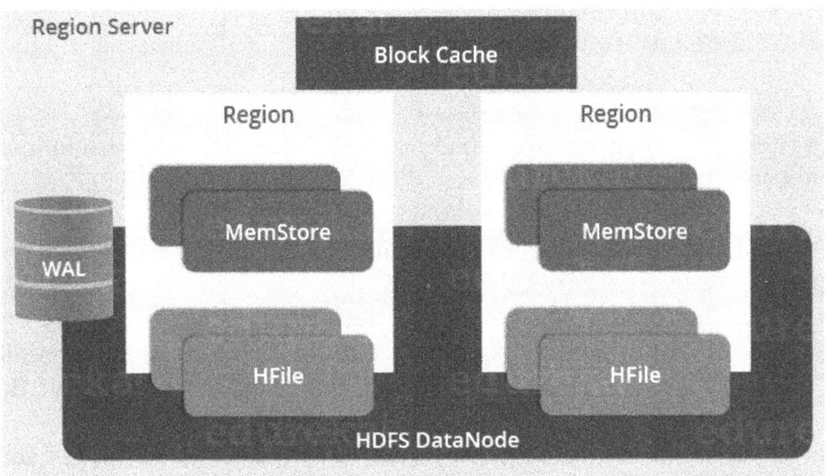

A Region Server maintains various regions running on the top of ***HDFS***. Components of a Region Server are:

1. **WAL:** As you can conclude from the above image, Write Ahead Log (WAL) is a file attached to every Region Server inside the distributed environment. The WAL stores the new data that hasn't been persisted or committed to the permanent storage. It is used in case of failure to recover the data sets.
2. **Block Cache:** From the above image, it is clearly visible that Block Cache resides in the top of Region Server. It stores the frequently read data in the memory. If the data in BlockCache is least recently used, then that data is removed from BlockCache.
3. **MemStore:** It is the write cache. It stores all the incoming data before committing it to the disk or permanent memory. There is one MemStore for each column family in a region. As you can see in the image, there are multiple MemStores for a region because each region contains multiple column families. The data is sorted in lexicographical order before committing it to the disk.
4. **HFile:** From the above figure you can see HFile is stored on HDFS. Thus, it stores the actual cells on the disk. MemStore commits the data to HFile when the size of MemStore exceeds.

How Search Initializes in HBase?

As you know, Zookeeper stores the META table location. Whenever a client approaches with a read or writes requests to HBase following operation occurs:

1. The client retrieves the location of the META table from the ZooKeeper.
2. The client then requests for the location of the Region Server of corresponding row key from the META table to access it. The client caches this information with the location of the META Table.
3. Then it will get the row location by requesting from the corresponding Region Server.

For future references, the client uses its cache to retrieve the location of META table and previously read row key's Region Server. Then the client will not refer to the META table, until and unless there is a miss because the region is shifted or moved. Then it will again request to the META server and update the cache.

3.3.5 HBase Write Mechanism

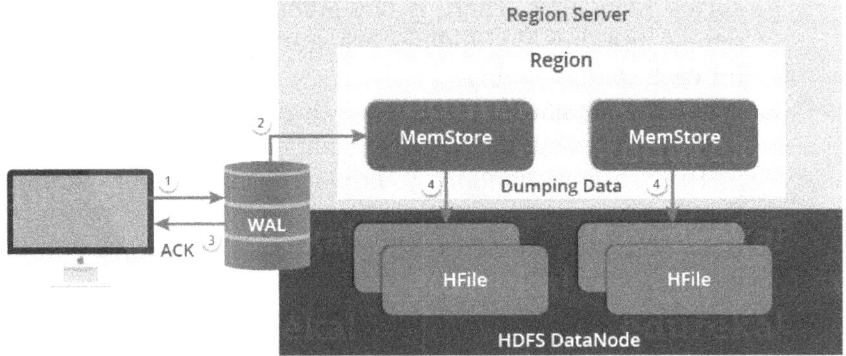

Step 1: The client sends a write data request to the HRegionServer through the scheduling of the Zookeeper, and writes the data in the HRegion.

Step 2: The data is written to the MemStore of HRegion until the MemStore reaches the preset threshold.

Step 3: The data in MemStore is Flushed into a StoreFile.

Step 4: As the number of StoreFile files increases, when the number of the StoreFile files increases to a certain threshold, the Compact merge operation is triggered, and multiple StoreFiles are merged into one StoreFile, and version merge and data deletion are performed at the same time.

Step 5: StoreFiles gradually forms a larger and larger StoreFile through the continuous Compact operation.

Step 6: After the size of a single StoreFile exceeds a certain threshold, the Split operation is triggered to split the current HRegion into two new HRegions. The parent HRegion will go offline, and the two sub-

HRegions from the new Split will be assigned to the corresponding HRegionServer by HMaster so that the pressure of the original HRegion can be shunted to the two HRegions.

HBase Write Mechanism- MemStore

1. The MemStore always updates the data stored in it, in a lexicographical order (sequentially in a dictionary manner) as sorted KeyValues. There is one MemStore for each column family, and thus the updates are stored in a sorted manner for each column family.
2. When the MemStore reaches the threshold, it dumps all the data into a new HFile in a sorted manner. This HFile is stored in HDFS. HBase contains multiple HFiles for each Column Family.
3. Over time, the number of HFile grows as MemStore dumps the data.
4. MemStore also saves the last written sequence number, so Master Server and MemStore both knows, that what is committed so far and where to start from. When region starts up, the last sequence number is read, and from that number, new edits start.

As discussed several times, that HFile is the main persistent storage in an HBase architecture. At last, all the data is committed to HFile which is the permanent storage of HBase. Hence, let us look at the properties of HFile which makes it faster for search while reading and writing.

HBase Write Mechanism- HFile

1. The writes are placed sequentially on the disk. Therefore, the movement of the disk's read-write head is very less. This makes write and search mechanism very fast.
2. The HFile indexes are loaded in memory whenever an HFile is opened. This helps in finding a record in a single seek.
3. The trailer is a pointer which points to the HFile's meta block. It is written at the end of the committed file. It contains information about timestamp and bloom filters.
4. Bloom Filter helps in searching key value pairs, it skips the file which does not contain the required row key. Timestamp

also helps in searching a version of the file, it helps in skipping the data.

After knowing the write mechanism and the role of various components in making write and search faster, we will explain how the reading mechanism works inside an HBase architecture? Then we will move to the mechanisms which increases HBase performance like compaction, region split and recovery.

Read Operation Flow

Step 1: The client accesses Zookeeper, finds the -ROOT-table, and obtains the .META. table information.

Step 2: Search from the .META. table to obtain the HRegion information of the target data, to find the corresponding HRegionServer.

Step 3: Obtain the data you need to find through HRegionServer.

Step 4: The memory of the HRegionserver is divided into two parts: MemStore and BlockCache. MemStore is mainly used to write data, and BlockCache is mainly used to read data. Read the request first to the MemStore to check the data, check the BlockCache check, and then check the StoreFile, and put the read result into the BlockCache.

3.3.6 Pre-Installation Setup

Before installing Hadoop into Linux environment, we need to set up Linux using **ssh** (Secure Shell). Follow the steps given below for setting up the Linux environment.

Creating a User

First of all, it is recommended to create a separate user for Hadoop to isolate the Hadoop file system from the Unix file system. Follow the steps given below to create a user.

- Open the root using the command “su”.
- Create a user from the root account using the command “useradd username”.
- Now you can open an existing user account using the comm-

nd "su username".

Open the Linux terminal and type the following commands to create a user.

$ su
password:
 # useradd hadoop
 # passwd hadoop
New passwd:
Retype new passwd

SSH Setup and Key Generation

SSH setup is required to perform different operations on the cluster such as start, stop, and distributed daemon shell operations. To authenticate different users of Hadoop, it is required to provide public/private key pair for a Hadoop user and share it with different users.

The following commands are used to generate a key value pair using SSH. Copy the public keys form id_rsa.pub to authorized_keys, and provide owner, read and write permissions to authorized_keys file respectively.

$ ssh-keygen -t rsa
$ cat ~/.ssh/id_rsa.pub >> ~/.ssh/authorized_keys
$ chmod 0600 ~/.ssh/authorized_keys

Verify ssh

ssh localhost

Installing Java

Java is the main prerequisite for Hadoop and HBase. First of all, you should verify the existence of java in your system using "java -version". The syntax of java version command is given below.

$ java -version

If everything works fine, it will give you the following output.

java version "1.7.0_71"

Java(TM) SE Runtime Environment (build 1.7.0_71-b13)
Java HotSpot(TM) Client VM (build 25.0-b02, mixed mode)

If java is not installed in your system, then follow the steps given below for installing java.

Step 1

Download java (JDK <latest version> - X64.tar.gz) by visiting the following link Oracle Java.

Then **jdk-7u71-linux-x64.tar.gz** will be downloaded into your system.

Step 2

Generally, you will find the downloaded java file in Downloads folder. Verify it and extract the **jdk-7u71-linux-x64.gz** file using the following commands.

```
$ cd Downloads/
$ ls
jdk-7u71-linux-x64.gz
$ tar zxf jdk-7u71-linux-x64.gz
$ ls
jdk1.7.0_71 jdk-7u71-linux-x64.gz
```

Step 3

To make java available to all the users, you have to move it to the location "/usr/local/". Open root and type the following commands.

```
$ su
password:
# mv jdk1.7.0_71 /usr/local/
# exit
```

Step 4

For setting up **PATH** and **JAVA_HOME** variables, add the following commands to **~/.bashrc** file.

export JAVA_HOME=/usr/local/jdk1.7.0_71
export PATH= $PATH:$JAVA_HOME/bin

Now apply all the changes into the current running system.

$ source ~/.bashrc

Step 5

Use the following commands to configure java alternatives

 # alternatives --install /usr/bin/java java usr/local/java/bin/java 2
 # alternatives --install /usr/bin/javac javac usr/local/java/bin/javac 2
 # alternatives --install /usr/bin/jar jar usr/local/java/bin/jar 2
 # alternatives --set java usr/local/java/bin/java
 # alternatives --set javac usr/local/java/bin/javac
 # alternatives --set jar usr/local/java/bin/jar

Now verify the **java -version** command from the terminal as explained above.

1. After installing java, you have to install Hadoop. First of all, verify the existence of Hadoop using " Hadoop version " command as shown below.
   Hadoop Version

2. If everything works fine, it will give you the following output.
   Hadoop 2.6.0
   Compiled by jenkins on 2014-11-13T21:10Z
   Compiled with protoc 2.5.0
   From source with checksum 18e43357c8f927c0695f1e9522859d6a
   This command was run using /home/hadoop/hadoop/share/hadoop/common/hadoop-common-2.6.0.jar

If your system is unable to locate Hadoop, then download Hadoop in your system. Follow the commands given below to do so,

Download and extract hadoop-2.6.0 from Apache Software Foundation using the following commands.

```
$ su
password:
# cd /usr/local
#                                                          wget
http://mirrors.advancedhosters.com/apache/hadoop/common/hado
op-
2.6.0/hadoop-2.6.0-src.tar.gz
# tar xzf hadoop-2.6.0-src.tar.gz
# mv hadoop-2.6.0/* hadoop/
# exit
```

Installing Hadoop

Install Hadoop in any of the required mode. Here, we are demonstrating HBase functionalities in pseudo distributed mode, therefore install Hadoop in pseudo distributed mode.

The following steps are used for installing **Hadoop 2.4.1**.

Step 1 - Setting up Hadoop

You can set Hadoop environment variables by appending the following commands to **~/.bashrc** file.

```
export HADOOP_HOME=/usr/local/hadoop
export HADOOP_MAPRED_HOME=$HADOOP_HOME
export HADOOP_COMMON_HOME=$HADOOP_HOME
export HADOOP_HDFS_HOME=$HADOOP_HOME
export YARN_HOME=$HADOOP_HOME
export HA-
DOOP_COMMON_LIB_NATIVE_DIR=$HADOOP_HOME/lib/native
export PATH=$PATH:$HADOOP_HOME/sbin:$HADOOP_HOME/bin
export HADOOP_INSTALL=$HADOOP_HOME
```

Now apply all the changes into the current running system.

$ source ~/.bashrc

Step 2 - Hadoop Configuration

You can find all the Hadoop configuration files in the location "$HADOOP_HOME/etc/hadoop". You need to make changes in those configuration files according to your Hadoop infrastructure.

$ cd $HADOOP_HOME/etc/hadoop

In order to develop Hadoop programs in java, you have to reset the java environment variable in **hadoop-env.sh** file by replacing **JAVA_HOME** value with the location of java in your system.

export JAVA_HOME=/usr/local/jdk1.7.0_71

You will have to edit the following files to configure Hadoop.

core-site.xml

The **core-site.xml** file contains information such as the port number used for Hadoop instance, memory allocated for file system, memory limit for storing data, and the size of Read/Write buffers.

Open core-site.xml and add the following properties in between the <configuration> and </configuration> tags.

```
<configuration>
  <property>
    <name>fs.default.name</name>
    <value>hdfs://localhost:9000</value>
  </property>
</configuration>
```

hdfs-site.xml

The **hdfs-site.xml** file contains information such as the value of replication data, namenode path, and datanode path of your local file systems, where you want to store the Hadoop infrastructure.

Let us assume the following data.

dfs.replication (data replication value) = 1
(In the below given path /hadoop/ is the user name. hadoopinfra/hdfs/namenode is the directory created by hdfs file system.)
namenode path = //home/hadoop/hadoopinfra/hdfs/namenode
(hadoopinfra/hdfs/datanode is the directory created by hdfs file system.)
datanode path = //home/hadoop/hadoopinfra/hdfs/datanode

Open this file and add the following properties in between the <configuration>, </configuration> tags.

```
<configuration>
  <property>
    <name>dfs.replication</name >
    <value>1</value>
  </property>

  <property>
    <name>dfs.name.dir</name>
    <val-
ue>file:///home/hadoop/hadoopinfra/hdfs/namenode</value>
  </property>

  <property>
    <name>dfs.data.dir</name>
    <val-
ue>file:///home/hadoop/hadoopinfra/hdfs/datanode</value>
  </property>
</configuration>
```

Note: In the above file, all the property values are user-defined and you can make changes according to your Hadoop infrastructure.

yarn-site.xml

This file is used to configure yarn into Hadoop. Open the yarn-site.xml file and add the following property in between the <configuration$gt;, </configuration$gt; tags in this file.

```
<configuration>
  <property>
    <name>yarn.nodemanager.aux-services</name>
    <value>mapreduce_shuffle</value>
  </property>
</configuration>
```

mapred-site.xml

This file is used to specify which MapReduce framework we are using. By default, Hadoop contains a template of yarn-site.xml. First of all, it is required to copy the file from **mapred-site.xml.template** to **mapred-site.xml** file using the following command.

$ cp mapred-site.xml.template mapred-site.xml

Open **mapred-site.xml** file and add the following properties in between the <configuration> and </configuration> tags.

```
<configuration>
  <property>
    <name>mapreduce.framework.name</name>
    <value>yarn</value>
  </property>
</configuration>
```

Verifying Hadoop Installation

The following steps are used to verify the Hadoop installation.

Step 1 - Name Node Setup

Set up the namenode using the command "hdfs namenode -format" as follows.

$ cd ~
$ hdfs namenode -format

The expected result is as follows.

```
10/24/14 21:30:55 INFO namenode.NameNode: STARTUP_MSG:
/************************************************************
STARTUP_MSG: Starting NameNode
STARTUP_MSG: host = localhost/192.168.1.11
STARTUP_MSG: args = [-format]
STARTUP_MSG: version = 2.4.1
...
...
10/24/14 21:30:56 INFO common.Storage: Storage directory
/home/hadoop/hadoopinfra/hdfs/namenode has been successfully
formatted.
10/24/14 21:30:56 INFO namenode.NNStorageRetentionManager:
Going to
retain 1 images with txid >= 0
10/24/14 21:30:56 INFO util.ExitUtil: Exiting with status 0
10/24/14 21:30:56 INFO namenode.NameNode: SHUTDOWN_MSG:
/************************************************************
SHUTDOWN_MSG: Shutting down NameNode at lo-
calhost/192.168.1.11
************************************************************/
```

Step 2 - Verifying Hadoop dfs

The following command is used to start dfs. Executing this command will start your Hadoop file system.

```
$ start-dfs.sh
```

The expected output is as follows.

```
10/24/14 21:37:56
Starting namenodes on [localhost]
localhost: starting namenode, logging to /home/hadoop/hadoop-
2.4.1/logs/hadoop-hadoop-namenode-localhost.out
localhost: starting datanode, logging to /home/hadoop/hadoop-
2.4.1/logs/hadoop-hadoop-datanode-localhost.out
Starting secondary namenodes [0.0.0.0]
```

Step 3 - Verifying Yarn Script

The following command is used to start the yarn script. Executing this command will start your yarn daemons.

```
$ start-yarn.sh
```

The expected output is as follows.

```
starting yarn daemons
starting resourcemanager, logging to /home/hadoop/hadoop-2.4.1/logs/yarn-hadoop-resourcemanager-localhost.out
localhost: starting nodemanager, logging to /home/hadoop/hadoop-2.4.1/logs/yarn-hadoop-nodemanager-localhost.out
```

Step 4 - Accessing Hadoop on Browser

The default port number to access Hadoop is 50070. Use the following url to get Hadoop services on your browser.

http://localhost:50070

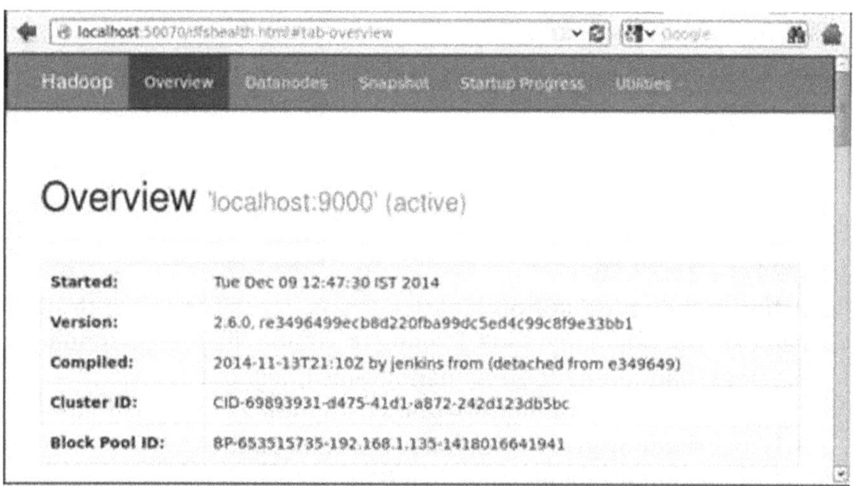

Step 5 - Verify all Applications of Cluster

The default port number to access all the applications of cluster is 8088. Use the following url to visit this service.

http://localhost:8088/

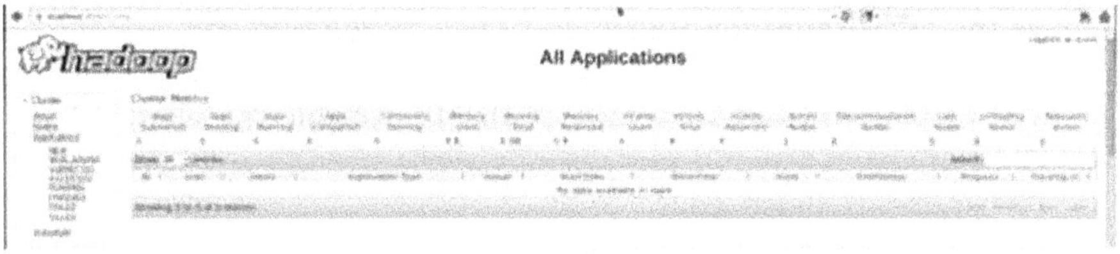

Installing HBase

We can install HBase in any of the three modes: Standalone mode, Pseudo Distributed mode, and Fully Distributed mode.

Installing HBase in Standalone Mode

Download the latest stable version of HBase form http://www.interior-dsgn.com/apache/hbase/stable/ using "wget" command, and extract it using the tar "zxvf" command. See the following command.

```
$cd usr/local/
$wget http://www.interior-dsgn.com/apache/hbase/stable/hbase-
0.98.8-
hadoop2-bin.tar.gz
$tar -zxvf hbase-0.98.8-hadoop2-bin.tar.gz
```

Shift to super user mode and move the HBase folder to /usr/local as shown below.

```
$su
$password: enter your password here
mv hbase-0.99.1/* Hbase/
```

Configuring HBase in Standalone Mode

Before proceeding with HBase, you have to edit the following files and configure HBase.

hbase-env.sh

Set the java Home for HBase and open **hbase-env.sh** file from the conf folder. Edit JAVA_HOME environment variable and change the existing path to your current JAVA_HOME variable as shown below.

```
cd /usr/local/Hbase/conf
gedit hbase-env.sh
```

This will open the env.sh file of HBase. Now replace the existing **JAVA_HOME** value with your current value as shown below.

```
export JAVA_HOME=/usr/lib/jvm/java-1.7.0
```

hbase-site.xml

This is the main configuration file of HBase. Set the data directory to an appropriate location by opening the HBase home folder in /usr/local/HBase. Inside the conf folder, you will find several files, open the **hbase-site.xml** file as shown below.

```
#cd /usr/local/HBase/
#cd conf
# gedit hbase-site.xml
```

Inside the **hbase-site.xml** file, you will find the <configuration> and </configuration> tags. Within them, set the HBase directory under the property key with the name "hbase.rootdir" as shown below.

```
<configuration>
  //Here you have to set the path where you want HBase to store its files.
  <property>
    <name>hbase.rootdir</name>
    <value>file:/home/hadoop/HBase/HFiles</value>
  </property>
```

```
  //Here you have to set the path where you want HBase to store its
built in zookeeper files.
  <property>
    <name>hbase.zookeeper.property.dataDir</name>
    <value>/home/hadoop/zookeeper</value>
  </property>
</configuration>
```

With this, the HBase installation and configuration part is successfully complete. We can start HBase by using **start-hbase.sh** script provided in the bin folder of HBase. For that, open HBase Home Folder and run HBase start script as shown below.

```
$cd /usr/local/HBase/bin
$./start-hbase.sh
```

If everything goes well, when you try to run HBase start script, it will prompt you a message saying that HBase has started.

starting master, logging to /usr/local/HBase/bin/../logs/hbase-tpmaster-localhost.localdomain.out

Installing HBase in Pseudo-Distributed Mode

Let us now check how HBase is installed in pseudo-distributed mode.

Configuring HBase

Before proceeding with HBase, configure Hadoop and HDFS on your local system or on a remote system and make sure they are running. Stop HBase if it is running.

hbase-site.xml

Edit hbase-site.xml file to add the following properties.

```
<property>
  <name>hbase.cluster.distributed</name>
  <value>true</value>
</property>
```

It will mention in which mode HBase should be run. In the same file from the local file system, change the hbase.rootdir, your HDFS instance address, using the hdfs://// URI syntax. We are running HDFS on the localhost at port 8030.

```
<property>
  <name>hbase.rootdir</name>
  <value>hdfs://localhost:8030/hbase</value>
</property>
```

Starting HBase

After configuration is over, browse to HBase home folder and start HBase using the following command.

```
$cd /usr/local/HBase
$bin/start-hbase.sh
```

Note: Before starting HBase, make sure Hadoop is running.

Checking the HBase Directory in HDFS

HBase creates its directory in HDFS. To see the created directory, browse to Hadoop bin and type the following command.

```
$ ./bin/hadoop fs -ls /hbase
```

If everything goes well, it will give you the following output.

```
Found 7 items
drwxr-xr-x - hbase users 0 2014-06-25 18:58 /hbase/.tmp
drwxr-xr-x - hbase users 0 2014-06-25 21:49 /hbase/WALs
drwxr-xr-x - hbase users 0 2014-06-25 18:48 /hbase/corrupt
drwxr-xr-x - hbase users 0 2014-06-25 18:58 /hbase/data
-rw-r--r-- 3 hbase users 42 2014-06-25 18:41 /hbase/hbase.id
-rw-r--r-- 3 hbase users 7 2014-06-25 18:41 /hbase/hbase.version
drwxr-xr-x - hbase users 0 2014-06-25 21:49 /hbase/oldWALs
```

Starting and Stopping a Master

Using the "local-master-backup.sh" you can start up to 10 servers. Open the home folder of HBase, master and execute the following command to start it.

$ ./bin/local-master-backup.sh 2 4

To kill a backup master, you need its process id, which will be stored in a file named **"/tmp/hbase-USER-X-master.pid."** you can kill the backup master using the following command.

$ cat /tmp/hbase-user-1-master.pid |xargs kill -9

Starting and Stopping RegionServers

You can run multiple region servers from a single system using the following command.

$ .bin/local-regionservers.sh start 2 3

To stop a region server, use the following command.

$ .bin/local-regionservers.sh stop 3

Starting HBaseShell

After Installing HBase successfully, you can start HBase Shell. Below given are the sequence of steps that are to be followed to start the HBase shell. Open the terminal, and login as super user.

Start Hadoop File System

Browse through Hadoop home sbin folder and start Hadoop file system as shown below.

$cd $HADOOP_HOME/sbin
$start-all.sh

Start HBase

Browse through the HBase root directory bin folder and start HBase.

$cd /usr/local/HBase
$./bin/start-hbase.sh

Start HBase Master Server

This will be the same directory. Start it as shown below.

$./bin/local-master-backup.sh start 2 (number signifies specific server.)

Start Region

Start the region server as shown below.

$./bin/./local-regionservers.sh start 3

Start HBase Shell

You can start HBase shell using the following command.
$cd bin
$./hbase shell

This will give you the HBase Shell Prompt as shown below.

2014-12-09 14:24:27,526 INFO [main] Configuration.deprecation: hadoop.native.lib is deprecated. Instead, use io.native.lib.available
HBase Shell; enter 'help<RETURN>' for list of supported commands.
Type "exit<RETURN>" to leave the HBase Shell
Version 0.98.8-hadoop2, r6cfc8d064754251365e070a10a82eb169956d5fe, Fri Nov 14 18:26:29 PST 2014
hbase(main):001:0>
HBase Web Interface

To access the web interface of HBase, type the following url in the browser.

http://localhost:60010

This interface lists your currently running Region servers, backup masters and HBase tables.

HBase Region servers and Backup Masters

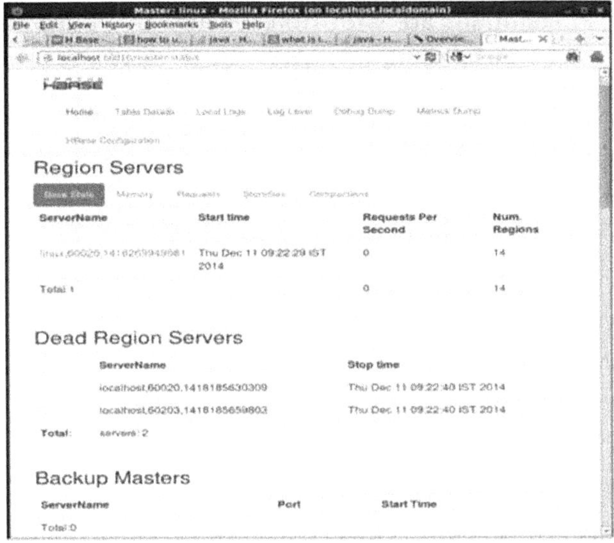

HBase Tables

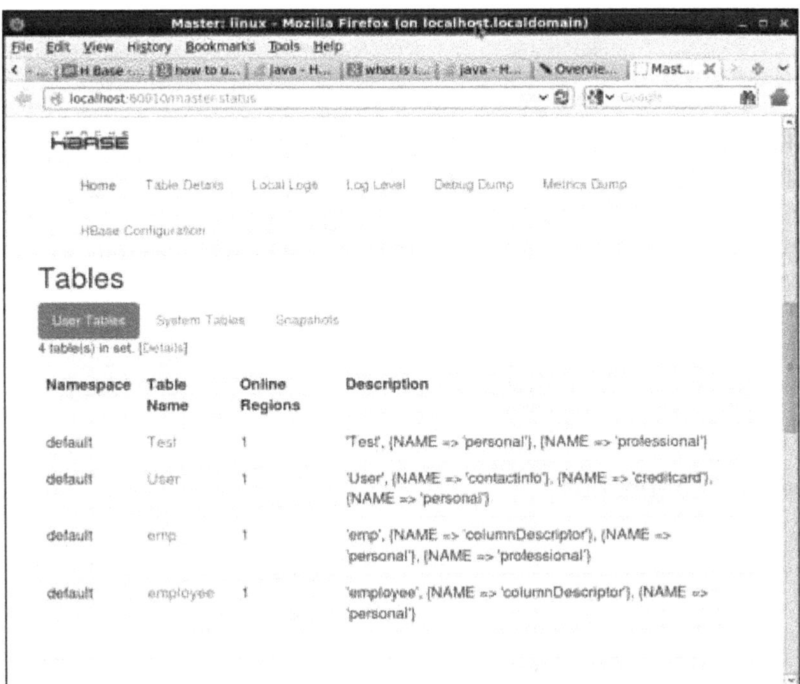

Setting Java Environment

We can also communicate with HBase using Java libraries, but before accessing HBase using Java API you need to set classpath for those libraries.

Setting the Classpath

Before proceeding with programming, set the classpath to HBase libraries in **.bashrc** file. Open **.bashrc** in any of the editors as shown below.

$ gedit ~/.bashrc

Set classpath for HBase libraries (lib folder in HBase) in it as shown below.

export CLASSPATH = $CLASSPATH://home/hadoop/hbase/lib/*

This is to prevent the "class not found" exception while accessing the HBase using java API.

HBase Shell

HBase contains a shell using which you can communicate with HBase. HBase uses the Hadoop File System to store its data. It will have a master server and region servers. The data storage will be in the form of regions (tables). These regions will be split up and stored in region servers.

The master server manages these region servers and all these tasks take place on HDFS. Given below are some of the commands supported by HBase Shell.

General Commands

- **status** - Provides the status of HBase, for example, the number of servers.
- **version** - Provides the version of HBase being used.
- **table_help** - Provides help for table-reference commands.
- **whoami** - Provides information about the user.

Data Definition Language

These are the commands that operate on the tables in HBase.

- **create** - Creates a table.
- **list** - Lists all the tables in HBase.
- **disable** - Disables a table.
- **is_disabled** - Verifies whether a table is disabled.
- **enable** - Enables a table.
- **is_enabled** - Verifies whether a table is enabled.
- **describe** - Provides the description of a table.
- **alter** - Alters a table.
- **exists** - Verifies whether a table exists.
- **drop** - Drops a table from HBase.
- **drop_all** - Drops the tables matching the 'regex' given in the command.
- **Java Admin API** - Prior to all the above commands, Java provides an Admin API to achieve DDL functionalities through programming. Under **org.apache.hadoop.hbase.client** package, HBaseAdmin and HTableDescriptor are the two important classes in this package that provide DDL functionalities.

Data Manipulation Language

- **put** - Puts a cell value at a specified column in a specified row in a particular table.
- **get** - Fetches the contents of row or a cell.
- **delete** - Deletes a cell value in a table.
- **deleteall** - Deletes all the cells in a given row.
- **scan** - Scans and returns the table data.
- **count** - Counts and returns the number of rows in a table.
- **truncate** - Disables, drops, and recreates a specified table.
- **Java client API** - Prior to all the above commands, Java provides a client API to achieve DML functionalities, **CRUD** (Create Retrieve Update Delete) operations and more through programming, under org.apache.hadoop.hbase.client package. **HTable Put** and **Get** are the important classes in this package.

Starting HBase Shell

To access the HBase shell, you have to navigate to the HBase home folder.

cd /usr/localhost/
cd Hbase

You can start the HBase interactive shell using **"hbase shell"** command as shown below.

./bin/hbase shell

If you have successfully installed HBase in your system, then it gives you the HBase shell prompt as shown below.

HBase Shell; enter 'help<RETURN>' for list of supported commands.

Type "exit<RETURN>" to leave the HBase Shell
Version 0.94.23, rf42302b28aceaab773b15f234aa8718fff7eea3c, Wed Aug 27
00:54:09 UTC 2014
hbase(main):001:0>

To exit the interactive shell command at any moment, type exit or use <ctrl+c>. Check the shell functioning before proceeding further. Use the **list** command for this purpose. **List** is a command used to get the list of all the tables in HBase. First of all, verify the installation and the configuration of HBase in your system using this command as shown below.

hbase(main):001:0> list

When you type this command, it gives you the following output.

hbase(main):001:0> list

table

The general commands in HBase are status, version, table_help, and whoami. This chapter explains these commands.

status

This command returns the status of the system including the details of the servers running on the system. Its syntax is as follows:

hbase(main):009:0> status

If you execute this command, it returns the following output.

hbase(main):009:0> status
3 servers, 0 dead, 1.3333 average load
version

This command returns the version of HBase used in your system. Its syntax is as follows:

hbase(main):010:0> version

If you execute this command, it returns the following output.

hbase(main):009:0> version
0.98.8-hadoop2, r6cfc8d064754251365e070a10a82eb169956d5fe, Fri Nov 14
18:26:29 PST 2014
table_help

This command guides you what and how to use table-referenced commands. Given below is the syntax to use this command.

hbase(main):02:0> table_help

When you use this command, it shows help topics for table-related commands. Given below is the partial output of this command.

hbase(main):002:0> table_help
Help for table-reference commands.
You can either create a table via 'create' and then manipulate the table via commands like 'put', 'get', etc. See the standard help information for how to use each of these commands. However, you can also

get a reference to a table, on which you can invoke commands. For instance, you can get create a table and keep around a reference to it via,

hbase> t = create 't', 'cf'......

whoami

This command returns the user details of HBase. If you execute this command, returns the current HBase user as shown below.

hbase(main):008:0> whoami
hadoop (auth:SIMPLE)
groups: Hadoop

3.4 Combining HBase and HDFS

Hadoop Distributed File System (HDFS), and Hbase (Hadoop database) are key components of Big Data ecosystem. This blog explains the difference between HDFS and HBase with real-life use cases where they are best fit.

The sudden increase in the volume of data from the order of gigabytes to zettabytes has created the need for a more organized file system for storage and processing of data. The demand stemming from the data market has brought Hadoop in the limelight making it one of biggest players in the industry. Hadoop Distributed File System (HDFS), the commonly known file system of Hadoop and Hbase (Hadoop's database) are the most topical and advanced data storage and management systems available in the market.

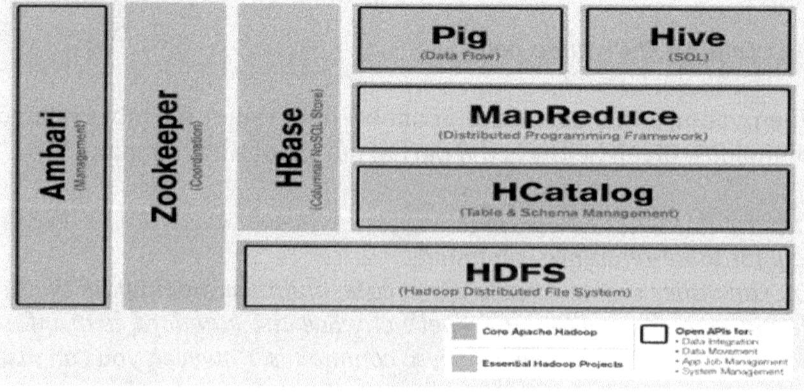

What are HDFS and HBase?

HDFS is fault-tolerant by design and supports rapid data transfer between nodes even during system failures. HBase is a non-relational and open source Not-Only-SQL database that runs on top of Hadoop. HBase comes under CP type of CAP (Consistency, Availability, and Partition Tolerance) theorem.

HDFS is most suitable for performing batch analytics. However, one of its biggest drawbacks is its inability to perform real-time analysis, the trending requirement of the IT industry. HBase, on the other hand, can handle large data sets and is not appropriate for batch analytics. Instead, it is used to write/read data from Hadoop in real-time.

Both HDFS and HBase are capable of processing structured, semi-structured as well as un-structured data. HDFS lacks an in-memory processing engine slowing down the process of data analysis; as it is using plain old MapReduce to do it. HBase, on the contrary, boasts of an in-memory processing engine that drastically increases the speed of read/write.

HDFS is very transparent in its execution of data analysis. HBase, on the other hand, being a NoSQL database in tabular format, fetches values by sorting them under different key values.

Enhanced Understanding with Use Cases for HDFS & HBase

Use Case 1 - Cloudera optimization for European bank using HBase

HBase is ideally suited for real-time environments and this can be best demonstrated by citing the example of our client, a renowned European bank. To derive critical insights from the logs from application/web servers, we implemented solution in Apache Storm and Apache Hbase together. Given the huge velocity of data, we opted for HBase over HDFS; as HDFS does not support real-time writes. The results were overwhelming; it reduced the query time from 3 days to 3 minutes.

Use Case 2 – Analytics solution for global CPG player using HDFS & MapReduce

With our global beverage player client, the primary objective was to perform batch analytics to gain SKU level insights, and involved recursive/sequential calculations.

DFS and MapReduce frameworks were better suited than complex Hive queries on top of Hbase. MapReduce was used for data wrangling and to prepare data for subsequent analytics. Hive was used for custom analytics on top of data processed by MapReduce. The results were impressive; as there was a drastic reduction in the time taken to generate custom analytics – 3 days to 3 hours.

UNIT 4

BIG DATA TECHNOLOGY LANDSCAPE AND HADOOP

In 2012 Gartner defined Big Data as follows "Big Data are high volume, high velocity, and/or high variety information assets that require new forms of processing to enable enhanced decision making, insight discovery and process optimization". Using a big data platform allows one to address the full spectrum of big data challenges. These platforms make use of traditional technologies that are most suited for structured and repeatable task and incorporate them with complementary new technologies that address speed and flexibility and are ideal for unstructured analysis as well as data exploration and discovery.

Data that sit unused are no different from data that were never collected in the first place
Doug Fisher

4.1 Introduction

Open platforms are software systems which have fully documented external application programming interface which allow the use of software in other ways than the original programmer intended without affecting the source code. Open platforms are based on open standards and does not mean they are open source.

Big data open platforms are based on similar concepts and various platforms are discussed that provide visualization and discovery of large data sets, monitors big data systems and speeds time to value with analytical and industry specific modules.

Exquisite Example "THE GOD PARTICLE"

An exquisite example of the enormous amount of data generator is The Large Hadron Collider which represent about of 150 million sensors delivers 150 million petabytes annual rate or nearly 500 exabytes per day. To put the numbers in perspective this is equivalent to 5×1020 bytes per day.

Almost 200 times higher than all the sources combined together in the world. To handle this huge chunk of data will be hard with the existing data management technologies. Hence the technology transitions have become imminent.

Technology Transition

With the introduction of Big Data platforms there has been a change in analytic techniques of organizations. The focus of the organizations has moved from orthodox methods like trend analysis and forecasting using historic data to its complementary and far better data visualization techniques. More interests had been shown towards scenario simulation and development over standardized reporting techniques. Analytics is emerging as a key to enhance business processes.

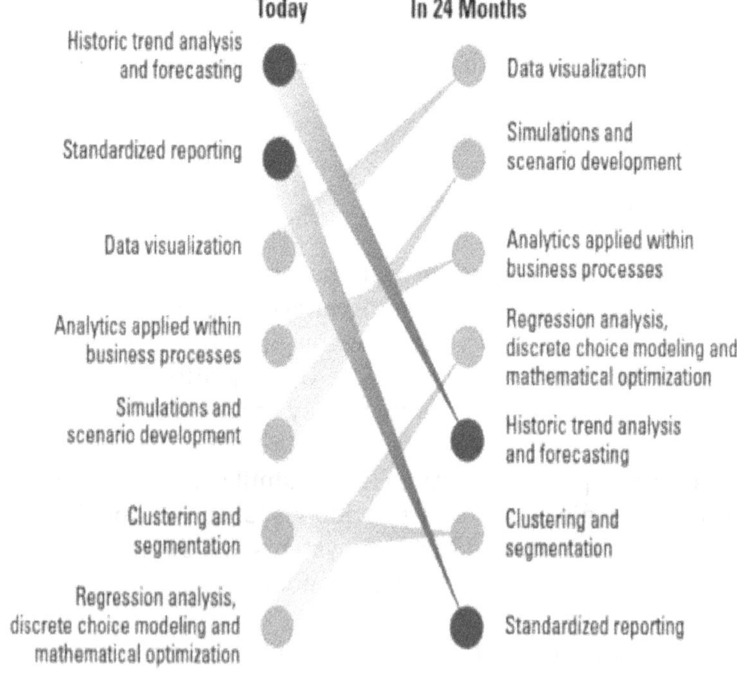

4.2 Classification of Big Data Tools

The Big Data tools landscape is growing rapidly, and they can be classified majorly into following areas:

1. Data Analysis
2. Databases/Data warehousing
3. Operational
4. Multi value Database
5. Business Intelligence
6. Data Mining
7. Key Value
8. Document Store
9. Graphs
10. Grid Solutions
11. Object Databases
12. Multi Model
13. XML databases
14. Big Data Search

There are many products available for each classification, which have their own special features to meet the requirements.

4.2.1 Big Data Landscape

In order to plan a big data architecture, it is important to grasp the knowledge of the current big data landscape and incorporate it into existing infrastructure.

In traditional data management structures, the structured information or data was fed into the enterprise integration tool which transferred the collected structured data into data warehouses or operational units.

Then different analytical capabilities were used to reveal the data, but the new form of data management structures that inherit big data landscape are designed to meet the velocity, volume, value and variety of requirements. To handle these large data sets, new architectures have been formed that incorporate multi node parallel processing techniques.

Big data landscape has a further classification based on processing requirements and different strategies are proposed for batch processing and real-time processing. Different technologies through which we can harness big data are:

1. Relational Database Management Systems
2. Massively Parallel Processing
3. MapReduce
4. NoSQL
5. Cassandra
6. Common Event Processing

Big Data Landscape

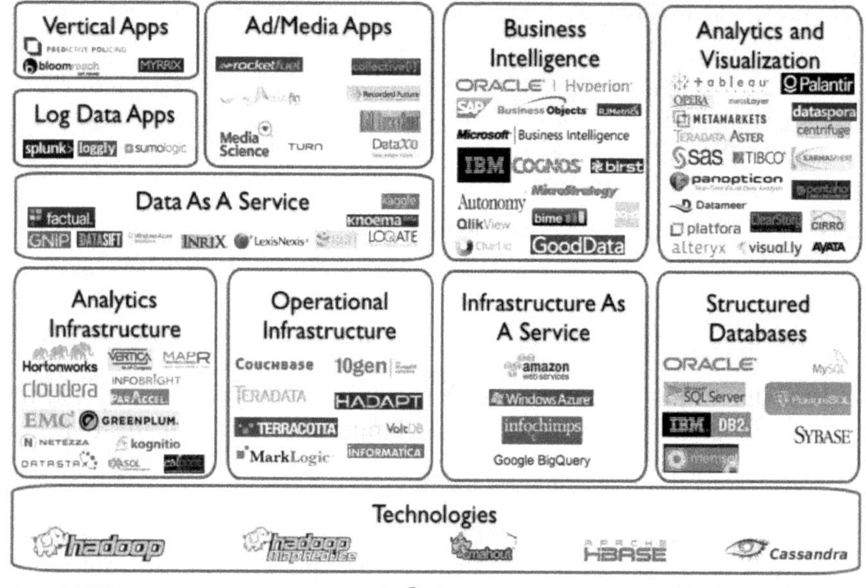

Copyright © 2012 Dave Feinleib dave@vcdave.com blogs.forbes.com/davefeinleib

Relational Database Management Systems

Databases are now using massively parallel processing techniques. These techniques are used to break data into small slots and to achieve faster processing operate them on multiple machines. Databases are acquiring columnar architecture to allow the storage of unstructured data.

Massively Parallel Processing

The data is distributed among a number of nodes for faster processing. The process is done parallel on each machine and the output is collected to deduce the required result. This technology requires knowledge of SQL and expensive hardware to work on.

MapReduce

Map reduce also use the concept of multi nodes and parallel processing. It consists of the following functions:

1. Map - It separates information over multiple nodes which are then processed in parallel.
2. Reduce - This function combines the result sets into a final response.
3. Massively parallel processing uses SQL queries whereas MapReduce uses java and does not need expensive dedicated platforms.

NoSQL

NoSQL database-management systems are unlike relational database-management systems, in that they do not use SQL as their query language. The idea behind these systems is that that they are better for handling data that doesn't fit easily into tables. They dispense with the overhead of indexing, schema and ACID transactional properties to create large, replicated data stores for running analytics on inexpensive hardware, which is useful for dealing with unstructured data.

4.3 Vendors

There is scarcely a vendor that doesn't have a big-data plan in train, with many companies combining their proprietary database products with the open-source Hadoop technology as their strategy to tackle velocity, variety and volume. Many of the early big-data technologies came out of open source, posing a threat to traditional IT vendors that have packaged their software and kept their intellectual property close to their chests. However, the open-source nature of the trend has also provided an opportunity for traditional IT vendors, because enterprise and government often find open-source tools off-putting.

Therefore, traditional vendors have welcomed Hadoop with open arms, packaging it in to their own proprietary systems so they can sell the result to enterprise as more comfortable and familiar packaged solutions.

1. CLOUDERA

Cloudera was founded in 2008 by employees who worked on Hadoop at Yahoo and Facebook. It contributes to the Hadoop open-source project, offering its own distribution of the software for free. It also sells a subscription-based, Hadoop-based distribution for the enterprise, which includes production support and tools to make it easier to run Hadoop.

Since its creation, various vendors have chosen Hadoop distribution for their own big-data products. In 2010, Teradata was one of the first to jump on the Cloudera bandwagon, with the two companies agreeing to connect the Hadoop distribution to Teradata's data warehouse so that customers could move information between the two. Around the same time, EMC made a similar arrangement for its Greenplum data warehouse. SGI and Dell signed agreements with Cloudera from the hardware side in 2011, while Oracle and IBM joined the party in 2012.

2. HORTONWORKS

Cloudera rival Hortonworks was birthed by key architects from the Yahoo Hadoop software engineering team. In June 2012, the company launched a high-availability version of Apache Hadoop, the Hortonworks Data Platform on which it collaborated with VMware, as the goal was to target companies deploying Hadoop on VMware's vSphere.

Teradata has also partnered with Hortonworks to create products that "help customers solve business problems in new and better ways".

3. TERADATA

Teradata made its move out of the "old-world" data- warehouse space by buying Aster Data Systems and Aprimo in 2011. Teradata wanted Aster's ability to manage "a variety of diverse data that is not structured", such as web applications, sensor networks, social networks, genomics, video and photographs.

Teradata has now gone to market with the Aster Data nCluster, a database using MPP and MapReduce. Visualization and analysis is enabled through the Aster Data visual- development environment and suite of analytic modules. The Hadoop connecter, enabled by its agreement with Cloudera, allows for a transfer of information between cluster and Hadoop.

4.4 Differences Between Apache Hadoop and RDBMS

Unlike Relational Database Management System (RDBMS), we cannot call Hadoop a database, but it is more of a distributed file system that can store and process a huge volume of data sets across a cluster of computers.

Hadoop has two major components: HDFS (Hadoop Distributed File System) and MapReduce. The former one is the storage layer of Hadoop which stores huge amounts of data. MapReduce is primarily a programming model which can effectively process the large data sets by converting them into different blocks of data. These blocks are distributed across the nodes on various machines in the cluster.

However, RDBMS is a structured database approach, in which data gets stored in tables in the forms of rows and columns. RDBMS uses SQL or Structured Query Language, which can help update and access the data present in different tables. As in the case of Hadoop, traditional RDBMS is not competent to be used in storage of a larger amount of data or simply big data.

Further, let's go through some of the major real-time working differences between the Hadoop database architecture and the traditional relational database management practices.

1. In Terms of Data Volume

Volume means the quantity of data which could be comfortably stored and effectively processed. Relational databases surely work better when the load is low, probably gigabytes of data. This was the case for so long in information technology applications, but when the data size has grown to Terabytes or Petabytes, RDBMS isn't competent to ensure the desired results. On the other hand, considering Hadoop is the right approach when the need is to handle a bigger data size. Hadoop can be used to process a huge volume of data effectively compared to the traditional relational database management systems.

2. Database Architecture

Considering the database architecture, as we have seen above Hadoop works on the components as:

- HDFS, which is the distributed file system of the Hadoop ecosystem.
- MapReduce, which is a programming model that help process huge data sets.
- Hadoop YARN, which helps in managing the computing resources in multiple clusters.

However, the traditional RDBMS will possess data based on the ACID properties, i.e., Atomicity, Consistency, Isolation, and Durability, which are used to maintain integrity and accuracy in data transactions. Such transactions would be of any sectors like banking systems, telecommunication, e-commerce, manufacturing, or education, etc.

3. Throughput

It is the total data volume process over a specific time period so that the output could be optimized.

Relational database management systems are found to be a failure in terms of achieving a higher throughput if the data volume is high, whereas Apache Hadoop Framework does an appreciable job in this regard. This is one major reason why there is an increasing usage of Hadoop in the modern-day data applications than RDBMS.

4. Data Diversity

The diversity of data refers to various types of data processed. There are structures, unstructured, and semi-structured data available now. Hadoop possesses a significant ability to store and process data of all the above-mentioned types and prepare it for processing. When it comes to processing big volume unstructured data, Hadoop is now the best-known solution.

However, traditional relational databases could only be used to manage structured or semi-structured data, in a limited volume. RDBMS fails in managing unstructured data. However, it is very difficult to fit in data from various sources to any proper structure. So, we can see that Hadoop is the apt solution in handling data diversity than RDBMS.

The other major areas we can compare also include the response time wherein RDBMS is a bit faster in retrieving information from a structured dataset. But, even though Hadoop has a higher throughput, the latency of Hadoop is comparatively Laser. Hadoop has a significant advantage of scalability compared to RDBMS. Ultimately, when it comes to the matter of cost Hadoop is fully free and open source, whereas RDBMS is more of licensed software, for which you need to pay.

4.5 Distributed Computing Challenges

Designing a distributed system does not come as easy and straight forward. A number of challenges need to be overcome in order to get the ideal system. The major challenges in distributed systems are listed below:

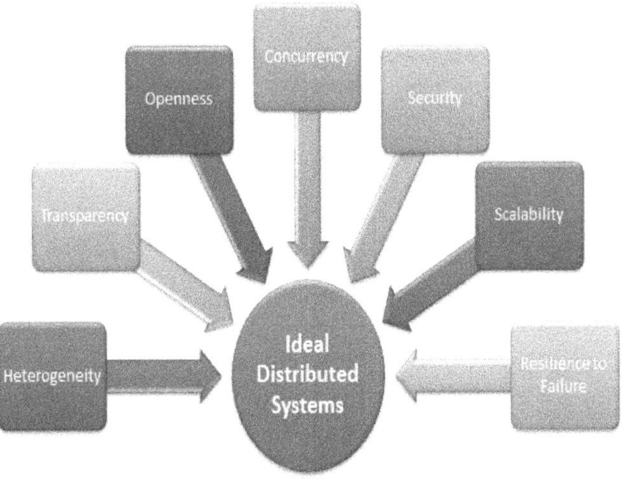

1. Heterogeneity

The Internet enables users to access services and run applications over a heterogeneous collection of computers and networks. Heterogeneity (that is, variety and difference) applies to all of the following:

a) Hardware devices: computers, tablets, mobile phones, embedded devices, etc.
b) Operating System: MS Windows, Linux, Mac, Unix, etc.
c) Network: Local network, the Internet, wireless network, satellite links, etc.
d) Programming languages: Java, C/C++, Python, PHP, etc.
e) Different roles of software developers, designers, system managers

Different programming languages use different representations for characters and data structures such as arrays and records. These differences must be addressed if programs written in different languages are to be able to communicate with one another. Programs written by different developers cannot communicate with one another unless they use common standards, for example, for network communication and the representation of primitive data items and data structures in messages.

Middleware

The term middleware applies to a software layer that provides a programming abstraction as well as masking the heterogeneity of the underlying networks, hardware, operating systems and programming languages. Most middleware is implemented over the Internet protocols, which themselves mask the differences of the underlying networks, but all middleware deals with the differences in operating systems and hardware.

Heterogeneity and mobile code

The term mobile code is used to refer to program code that can be transferred from one computer to another and run at the destination – Java applets are an example. Code suitable for running on one computer is not necessarily suitable for running on another because executable programs are normally specific both to the instruction set and to the host operating system.

2. Transparency

Transparency is defined as the concealment from the user and the application programmer of the separation of components in a distributed system, so that the system is perceived as a whole rather than as a collection of independent components. In other words, distributed systems designers must hide the complexity of the systems as much as they can.

Some terms of transparency in distributed systems are,

Access - Hide differences in data representation and how a resource is accessed
Location - Hide where a resource is located
Migration - Hide that a resource may move to another location
Relocation - Hide that a resource may be moved to another location while in use
Replication - Hide that a resource may be copied in several places
Concurrency - Hide that a resource may be shared by several competitive users
Failure - Hide the failure and recovery of a resource
Persistence - Hide whether a (software) resource is in memory

3. Openness

The openness of a computer system is the characteristic that determines whether the system can be extended and reimplemented in various ways. The openness of distributed systems is determined primarily by the degree to which new resource-sharing services can be added and be made available for use by a variety of client programs. If the well-defined interfaces for a system are published, it is easier for developers to add new features or replace sub-systems in the future. Example: Twitter and Facebook have API that allows developers to develop their own software interactively.

4. Concurrency

Both services and applications provide resources that can be shared by clients in a distributed system. There is therefore a possibility that several clients will attempt to access a shared resource at the same time. For example, a data structure that records bids for an auction may be accessed very frequently when it gets close to the deadline time. For an object to be safe in a concurrent environment, its operations must be synchronized in such a way that its data remains consistent. This can be achieved by standard techniques such as semaphores, which are used in most operating systems.

5. Security

Many of the information resources that are made available and maintained in distributed systems have a high intrinsic value to their users. Their security is therefore of considerable importance. Security for information resources has three components,

Confidentiality - protection against disclosure to unauthorized individuals
Integrity - protection against alteration or corruption
Availability - for the authorized, protection against interference with the means to access the resource

6. Scalability

Distributed systems must be scalable as the number of user increases. The scalability is defined by B. Clifford Neuman as,

A system is said to be scalable if it can handle the addition of users and resources without suffering a noticeable loss of performance or increase in administrative complexity

Scalability has 3 dimensions:

Size

Number of users and resources to be processed. Problem associated is overloading

Geography

Distance between users and resources. Problem associated is communication reliability

Administration

As the size of distributed systems increases, many of the system needs to be controlled. Problem associated is administrative mess

7. Failure Handling

Computer systems sometimes fail. When faults occur in hardware or software, programs may produce incorrect results or may stop before they have completed the intended computation. The handling of failures is particularly difficult.

4.6 History of Hadoop

Hadoop is an open-source framework overseen by Apache Software Foundation which is written in Java for storing and processing of huge datasets with the cluster of commodity hardware.

There are mainly two problems with the big data. First one is to store such a huge amount of data and the second one is to process that stored data. The traditional approach like RDBMS is not sufficient due to the heterogeneity of the data.

Thus, Hadoop comes as the solution to the problem of big data i.e., storing and processing the big data with some extra capabilities. There are mainly two components of Hadoop which are Hadoop Distributed File System (HDFS) **and** Yet Another Resource Negotiator (YARN).

2002 – 2004: Apache Nutch was started in the year 2002 by Doug Cutting which is an effort to build an open source web search engine based on Lucene and Java for the search and index component. Nutch was based on sort/merge processing. In June 2003, it was successfully demonstrated on 4 nodes by crawling 100 million pages. However, they realised that their architecture wouldn't scale to billions of pages on web. There comes the help with the publication of a paper in 2003 that described the architecture of the Google's Distributed Filesystem, called GFS which has been used in production at Google which would solve their storage needs for the very large files generated as part of the web crawling and indexing process.

2004 – 2006: In the year 2004, they started writing the open source implementation called Nutch Distributed Filesystem (NDFS). In the same year Google published a paper that introduces MapReduce to the world. Early in the year 2005, the Nutch developers had a working MapReduce Implementation in Nutch and by the middle of that year all the major Nutch algorithms had been ported using the MapReduce and NDFS (Nutch Distributed *FileSystem).* In Febraury, 2006 they moved out of Nutch to form an independent subproject of Lucene called Hadoop.

2004: Initial versions of what is now Hadoop Distributed FileSystem and MapReduce implemented by Doug Cutting and Mike Cafarella.

December 2005: Nutch ported to a new framework. Hadoop runs reliably on 20 nodes.

2006 - 2008: Doug Cutting joined Yahoo! in the year 2006, which provided him the dedicated team and resources to turn Hadoop in to a system that ran at web scale. Hadoop was made Apache's top-level project in the year 2008.

February 2006: Apache Hadoop project officially started to support the standalone development of MapReduce and HDFS.

February 2006: Adoption of Hadoop by Yahoo! Grid Team.

April 2006: Sort benchmark (10 GB/node) run on 188 nodes in 47.9.

May 2006: Yahoo! set up a Hadoop 300 nodes research cluster.

May 2006: Sort benchmark run on 500 nodes in 42 hours (better hardware than April benchmark)

October 2006: Research cluster reaches 600 nodes.

December 2006: Sort benchmark run on 20 nodes in 1.8 hours, 100 nodes in 3.3 hours, 500 nodes in 5.2 hours, 900 nodes in 7.8 hours.

January 2007: Research cluster reaches 900 nodes.

April 2007: Research clusters - two cluster of 1000 nodes.

April 2008: Won 1 Terabyte sort benchmark in 208 seconds on 990 nodes.

October 2008: Loading 10 Terabytes of data per day into research clusters.

2008 - now: After 2008 there is a full time development that is going on. There are many releases of Hadoop, you can find them here.

March 2009: 17 clusters with a total of 24,000 nodes.

April 2009: Won the minute sort by sorting 500 GB in 59 seconds on 1,400 nodes and 100 TB sort in 173 minutes on 3,400 nodes.

2011: Yahoo was running its search engine across 42,000 nodes.

July 2013: Sorting at a rate of 1.42 Terabytes per minute.

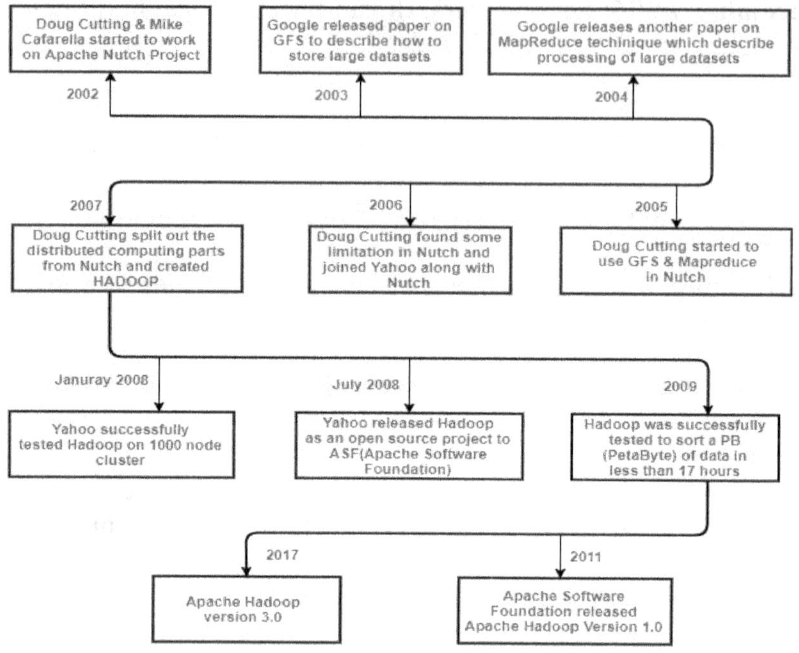
Doug Cutting & Mike Cafarella started to work on Apache Nutch Project
Google released paper on GFS to describe how to store large datasets
Google releases another paper on MapReduce techinique which describe processing of large datasets
2002
2003
2004
2007
2006
2005
Doug Cutting split out the distributed computing parts from Nutch and created HADOOP
Doug Cutting found some limitation in Nutch and joined Yahoo along with Nutch
Doug Cutting started to use GFS & Mapreduce in Nutch
Januray 2008
July 2008
2009
Yahoo successfully tested Hadoop on 1000 node cluster
Yahoo released Hadoop as an open source project to ASF(Apache Software Foundation)
Hadoop was successfully tested to sort a PB (PetaByte) of data in less than 17 hours
2017
2011
Apache Hadoop version 3.0
Apache Software Foundation released Apache Hadoop Version 1.0

4.7 Hadoop Overview

Hadoop is an open source framework managed by the Apache Software Foundation. Open source implies that it is freely available and its source code can be changed as per the user's requirements. Apache Hadoop is designed to store and process big data efficiently. Hadoop is used for data storing, processing, analyzing, accessing, governance, operations, and security.

Large organizations with a huge amount of data use Hadoop, processed with the help of a large cluster of commodity hardware. Cluster refers to a group of systems which are connected via LAN and multiple nodes on this cluster help in performing Hadoop jobs. Hadoop has gained popularity worldwide in managing big data and, at present, it has a nearly 90% market share.

4.7.1 Features of Hadoop

1. **Cost Effective**: Hadoop system is very cost effective as it does not require any specialized hardware and thus requires

low investment. Use of simple hardware known as commodity hardware is sufficient for the system.

2. **Supports Large Cluster of Nodes**: A Hadoop structure can be made of thousands of nodes making a large cluster. Large cluster helps in expanding the storage system & offers more computing power.
3. **Parallel Processing of Data**: Hadoop system supports parallel processing of the data across all nodes in the cluster, and thus it reduces the storage & processing time.
4. **Distribution of Data (Distributed Processing)**: Hadoop efficiently distributes the data across all the nodes in a cluster. Moreover, it replicates the data over the entire cluster in order to retrieve the data other nodes, if a particular node is busy or fails to operate.
5. **Automatic Failover Management (Fault Tolerance)**: An important feature of Hadoop is that it automatically resolves the problem in case a node in the cluster fails. The framework itself replaces the failed system with another system along with configuring the replicated settings and data on the new machine.
6. **Supports Heterogeneous Clusters**: A heterogeneous cluster is one which accounts for nodes or machines which are from a different vendor, different operating system, and running on different versions. For instance, if a Hadoop cluster has three systems, one Lenovo machine that runs on RHEL Linux, the second is Intel machine running on Ubuntu Linux, and third is an AMD machine running on Fedora Linux, all of these different systems are capable of simultaneously running on a single cluster.
7. **Scalability**: A Hadoop system has the ability to add or remove node/nodes and hardware components from a cluster, without affecting the operations of the cluster. This refers to scalability, which is one of the important features of the Hadoop system.

4.7.2 Hadoop Architecture

At its core, Hadoop has two major layers namely

- Processing/Computation layer (MapReduce), and
- Storage layer (Hadoop Distributed File System).

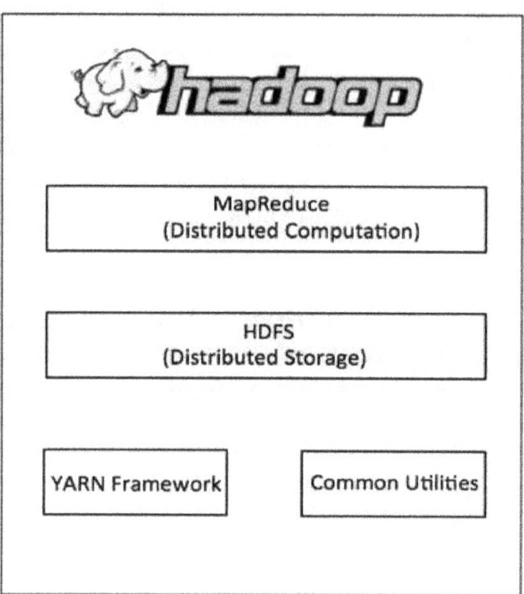

1. MapReduce: MapReduce is a parallel programming model for writing distributed applications devised at Google for efficient processing of large amounts of data (multi-terabyte data-sets), on large clusters (thousands of nodes) of commodity hardware in a reliable, fault-tolerant manner. The MapReduce program runs on Hadoop which is an Apache open-source framework.

2. Hadoop Distributed File System: The Hadoop Distributed File System (HDFS) is based on the Google File System (GFS) and provides a distributed file system that is designed to run on commodity hardware. It has many similarities with existing distributed file systems. However, the differences from other distributed file systems are significant. It is highly fault-tolerant and is designed to be deployed on low-cost hardware. It provides high throughput access to application data and is suitable for applications having large datasets.

Apart from the above-mentioned two core components, Hadoop framework also includes the following two modules,

3. Hadoop Common: These are Java libraries and utilities required by other Hadoop modules.

4. Hadoop YARN: This is a framework for job scheduling and cluster resource management.

4.7.3 How Does Hadoop Work?

It is quite expensive to build bigger servers with heavy configurations that handle large scale processing, but as an alternative, you can tie together many commodity computers with single-CPU, as a single functional distributed system and practically, the clustered machines can read the dataset in parallel and provide a much higher throughput.

Moreover, it is cheaper than one high-end server. So this is the first motivational factor behind using Hadoop that it runs across clustered and low-cost machines.

Hadoop runs code across a cluster of computers. This process includes the following core tasks that Hadoop performs,

1. Data is initially divided into directories and files. Files are divided into uniform sized blocks of 128M and 64M (preferably 128M).
2. These files are then distributed across various cluster nodes for further processing.
3. HDFS, being on top of the local file system, supervises the processing.
4. Blocks are replicated for handling hardware failure.
5. Checking that the code was executed successfully.
6. Performing the sort that takes place between the map and reduce stages.
7. Sending the sorted data to a certain computer.
8. Writing the debugging logs for each job.

Use Case of Hadoop: Hadoop is beginning to live up to its promise of being the backbone technology for Big Data storage and analytics. Companies across the globe have started to migrate their data into Hadoop to join the stalwarts who already adopted Hadoop a while ago. It is important to study and understand several Hadoop use cases for these simple reasons –

- Hadoop is still a complex technology with several limitations and complications.

- All Data is not Big Data and might not require a Hadoop solution.
- Companies that use Hadoop, often fall into the error of not using the right Hadoop architecture and tools, thereby reducing Hadoop's efficiency.

Studying Hadoop use cases will help to

1) Understand what kind of big data problems need Hadoop and
2) What sort of infrastructure should one have in order to set up and work on the Hadoop framework.

The two obvious benefits of using Hadoop is that, it provides storage for any kind of data from various sources and provides a platform for proficient analytics of the data with low latency.

Hadoop is well known to be a distributed, scalable and fault-tolerant system. It can store petabytes with relatively low infrastructure investment. Hadoop runs on clusters of commodity servers. All such servers have local storage and CPU which can store few terabytes on its local disk.

Here are five examples of Hadoop use cases:

1. Financial services companies use analytics to assess risk, build investment models, and create trading algorithms; Hadoop has been used to help build and run those applications.
2. Retailers use it to help analyze structured and unstructured data to better understand and serve their customers.
3. In the asset-intensive energy industry Hadoop-powered analytics are used for predictive maintenance, with input from Internet of Things (IoT) devices feeding data into big data programs.
4. Telecommunications companies can adapt all the aforementioned use cases. For example, they can use Hadoop-powered analytics to execute predictive maintenance on their infrastructure. Big data analytics can also plan efficient network paths and recommend optimal locations for new cell towers or other network expansion. To support custom-

er-facing operations Telcom can analyze customer behavior and billing statements to inform new service offerings.

5. There are numerous public sector programs, ranging from anticipating and preventing disease outbreaks to crunching numbers to catch tax cheats.

4.7.4 Hadoop Distributors

The Case for Distributions: Hadoop is Apache software so it is freely available for download and use. So why do we need distributions at all?

This is very akin to Linux a few years back and Linux distributions like RedHat, Suse and Ubuntu. The software is free to download and use but distributions offer an easier to use bundle.

So what does Hadoop distros offer?

Distributions provide easy to install mediums like RPMs

The Apache version of Hadoop is just TAR balls. Distros actually package it nicely into easy to install packages which make it easy for system administrators to manage effectively.

Distros package multiple components that work well together

The Hadoop ecosystem contains a lot of components (HBase, Pig, Hive, Zookeeper, etc.) which are being developed independently and have their own release schedules. Also, there are version dependencies among the components. For example, version 0.92 of HBase needs a particular version of HDFS. Distros bundle versions of components that work well together. This provides a working Hadoop installation right out of the box.

Tested: Distro makers strive to ensure good quality components.

Performance patches: Sometimes, distros lead the way by including performance patches to the 'vanilla' versions.

Predictable upgrade path: Distros have predictable product release road maps. This ensures they keep up with developments and bug fixes.

SUPPORT: Lot of distros come with support, which could be very valuable for a production critical cluster.

Hadoop Distributions

Distro	Remarks	Free / Premium
Apache hadoop.apache.org	The Hadoop Source No packaging except TAR balls No extra tools	Completely free and open source
Cloudera www.cloudera.com	Oldest distro Very polished Comes with good tools to install and manage a Hadoop cluster	Free / Premium model (depending on cluster size)
HortonWorks www.hortonworks.com	Newer distro Tracks Apache Hadoop closely Comes with tools to manage and administer a cluster	Completely open source
MapR www.mapr.com	MapR has their own file system (alternative to HDFS) Boasts higher performance Nice set of tools to manage and administer a cluster Does not suffer from Single Point of Failure Offer some cool features like mirroring, snapshots, etc.	Free / Premium model
Intel hadoop.intel.com	Encryption support Hardware acceleration added to some layers of stack to boost performance	Premium

Distro	Remarks	Free / Premium
	Admin tools to deploy and manage Hadoop	
Pivotal HD gopivotal.com	fast SQL on Hadoop software only or appliance	Premium

4.7.5 Hadoop in the Cloud

Elephants can really fly in the clouds! Most cloud providers offer Hadoop.

1. Hadoop clusters in the Cloud: Hadoop clusters can be set up in any cloud service that offers suitable machines. However, in line with the cloud mantra 'only pay for what you use', Hadoop can be run 'on demand' in the cloud.
2. Amazon Elastic Map Reduce: Amazon offers 'On Demand Hadoop', which means there is no permanent Hadoop cluster. A cluster is spun up to do a job and after that it is shut down - 'pay for usage. Amazon offers a slightly customized version of Apache Hadoop and also offers MapR's distribution.
3. Google's Compute Engine: Google offers MapR's Hadoop distribution in their Compute Engine Cloud.
4. SkyTab Cloud: SkyTap offers deployable Hadoop templates

4.7.6 Introduction to HDFS (Hadoop Distributed File System)

With growing data velocity, the data size easily outgrows the storage limit of a machine. A solution would be to store the data across a network of machines. Such filesystems are called distributed filesystems. Since data is stored across a network all the complications of a network come in.

This is where Hadoop comes in. It provides one of the most reliable filesystems. HDFS (Hadoop Distributed File System) is a unique design that provides storage for extremely large files with streaming data access pattern, and it runs on commodity hardware.

Hadoop File System was developed using distributed file system design. It is run on commodity hardware. Unlike other distributed systems, HDFS is highly faulttolerant and designed using low-cost hardware.

Features of HDFS

- It is suitable for the distributed storage and processing.
- Hadoop provides a command interface to interact with HDFS.
- The built-in servers of namenode and datanode help users to easily check the status of cluster.
- Streaming access to file system data.
- HDFS provides file permissions and authentication.

Let's elaborate the terms

- **Extremely large files**: Here we are talking about the data in range of petabytes (1000 TB).
- **Streaming Data Access Pattern**: HDFS is designed on principle of write-once and read-many-times. Once data is written large portions of dataset can be processed any number times.
- **Commodity hardware:** Hardware that is inexpensive and easily available in the market. This is one of feature which specially distinguishes HDFS from other file system.

Assumptions and Goals

Hardware Failure: Hardware failure is the norm rather than the exception. An HDFS instance may consist of hundreds or thousands of server machines, each storing part of the file system's data. The fact that there are a huge number of components and that each component has a non-trivial probability of failure means that some component of HDFS is always non-functional. Therefore, detection of faults and quick, automatic recovery from them is a core architectural goal of HDFS.

Streaming Data Access: Applications that run on HDFS need streaming access to their data sets. They are not general purpose applications that typically run on general purpose file systems. HDFS is designed more for batch processing rather than interactive use by users. The emphasis is on high throughput of data access rather than low latency of data access. POSIX imposes many hard requirements that are not needed for applications that are targeted for HDFS. POSIX semantics in a few key areas has been traded to increase data throughput rates.

Large Data Sets: Applications that run on HDFS have large data sets. A typical file in HDFS is gigabytes to terabytes in size. Thus, HDFS is tuned to support large files. It should provide high aggregate data bandwidth and scale to hundreds of nodes in a single cluster. It should support tens of millions of files in a single instance.

Simple Coherency Model: HDFS applications need a write-once-read-many access model for files. A file once created, written, and closed need not be changed. This assumption simplifies data coherency issues and enables high throughput data access. A MapReduce application or a web crawler application fits perfectly with this model. There is a plan to support appending-writes to files in the future.

Moving Computation is Cheaper than Moving Data: A computation requested by an application is much more efficient if it is executed near the data it operates on. This is especially true when the size of the data set is huge. This minimizes network congestion and increases the overall throughput of the system. The assumption is that it is often better to migrate the computation closer to where the data is located rather than moving the data to where the application is running. HDFS provides interfaces for applications to move themselves closer to where the data is located.

Portability Across Heterogeneous Hardware and Software Platforms: HDFS has been designed to be easily portable from one platform to another. This facilitates widespread adoption of HDFS as a platform of choice for a large set of applications.

4.7.7 HDFS Architecture

Given below is the architecture of a Hadoop File System.

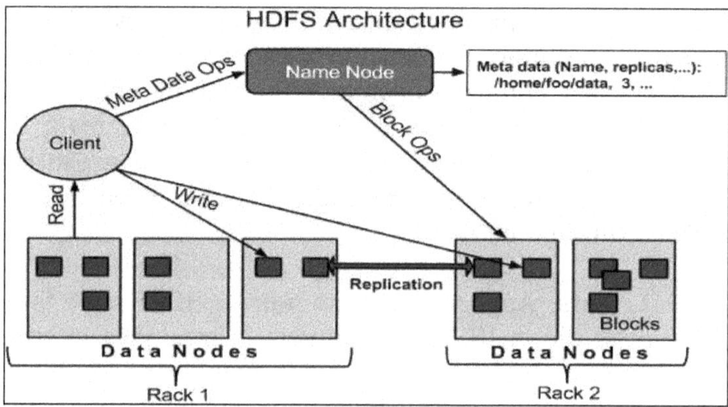

Nodes: Master-slave nodes typically forms the HDFS cluster.

1. MasterNode

- Manages all the slave nodes and assign work to them.
- It executes filesystem namespace operations like opening, closing, renaming files and directories.
- It should be deployed on reliable hardware which has the high config. not on commodity hardware.

2. NameNode

- Actual worker nodes, who do the actual work like reading, writing, processing etc.
- They also perform creation, deletion, and replication upon instruction from the master.

- They can be deployed on commodity hardware.

Block

Generally, the user data is stored in the files of HDFS. The file in a file system will be divided into one or more segments and/or stored in individual data nodes. These file segments are called as blocks. In other words, the minimum amount of data that HDFS can read or write is called a Block. The default block size is 64MB, but it can be increased as per the need to change in HDFS configuration.

Data storage in HDFS: Now let's see how the data is stored in a distributed manner.

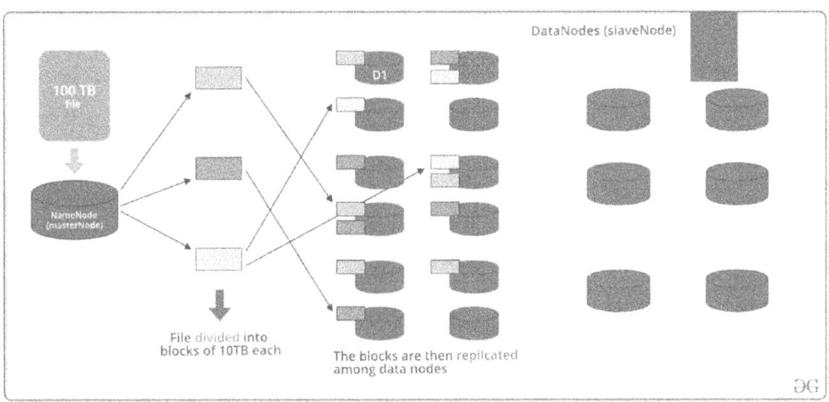

Lets assume that 100TB file is inserted, then masternode(namenode) will first divide the file into blocks of 10TB (default size is 128 MB in Hadoop 2.x and above). Then these blocks are stored across different datanodes(slavenode). Datanodes(slavenode)replicate the blocks among themselves and the information of what blocks they contain is sent to the master. Default replication factor is *3* means for each block 3 replicas are created (including itself). In hdfs.site.xml we can increase or decrease the replication factor i.e we can edit its configuration here.

Note: MasterNode has the record of everything, it knows the location and info of each and every single data node and the blocks they contain, i.e. nothing is done without the permission of masternode.

Why divide the file into blocks?

Let's assume that we don't divide, now it's very difficult to store a 100 TB file on a single machine. Even if we store, then each read and write operation on that whole file is going to take very high seek time. But if we have multiple blocks of size 128MB then its become easy to perform various read and write operations on it compared to doing it on a whole file at once. So we divide the file to have faster data access i.e. reduce seek time.

Why replicate the blocks in data nodes while storing?

Let's assume we don't replicate and only one yellow block is present on datanode D1. Now if the data node D1 crashes we will lose the block and which will make the overall data inconsistent and faulty. So we replicate the blocks to achieve fault-tolerance.

Terms related to HDFS:

1. **HeartBeat**: It is the signal that datanode continuously sends to namenode. If namenode doesn't receive heartbeat from a datanode then it will consider it dead.
2. **Balancing**: If a datanode is crashed the blocks present on it will be gone too and the blocks will be under-replicated compared to the remaining blocks. Here master node(namenode) will give a signal to datanodes containing replicas of those lost blocks to replicate so that overall distribution of blocks is balanced.
3. **Replication**: It is done by datanode

Limitations: Though HDFS provide many features there are some areas where it doesn't work well.

1. **Low latency data access**: Applications that require low-latency access to data i.e in the range of milliseconds will not work well with HDFS, because HDFS is designed keeping in mind that we need high-throughput of data even at the cost of latency.
2. **Small file problem**: Having lots of small files will result in lots of seeks and lots of movement from one datanode to an-

other datanode to retrieve each small file, this whole process is a very inefficient data access pattern.

4.7.8 Starting HDFS

Initially you have to format the configured HDFS file system, open namenode (HDFS server), and execute the following command.

$ hadoop namenode -format

After formatting the HDFS, start the distributed file system. The following command will start the namenode as well as the data nodes as cluster.

$ start-dfs.sh

1. Listing Files in HDFS

After loading the information in the server, we can find the list of files in a directory, status of a file, using **'ls'**. Given below is the syntax of **ls** that you can pass to a directory or a filename as an argument.

$ $HADOOP_HOME/bin/hadoop fs -ls <args>

2. Inserting Data into HDFS

Assume we have data in the file called file.txt in the local system which is ought to be saved in the hdfs file system. Follow the steps given below to insert the required file in the Hadoop file system.

Step 1

You have to create an input directory.

$ $HADOOP_HOME/bin/hadoop fs -mkdir /user/input

Step 2

Transfer and store a data file from local systems to the Hadoop file system using the put command.

$ $HADOOP_HOME/bin/hadoop fs -put /home/file.txt /user/input

Step 3

You can verify the file using ls command.

$ $HADOOP_HOME/bin/hadoop fs -ls /user/input

3. Retrieving Data from HDFS

Assume we have a file in HDFS called **outfile**. Given below is a simple demonstration for retrieving the required file from the Hadoop file system.

Step 1

Initially, view the data from HDFS using **cat** command.

$ $HADOOP_HOME/bin/hadoop fs -cat /user/output/outfile

Step 2

Get the file from HDFS to the local file system using **get** command.

$ $HADOOP_HOME/bin/hadoop fs -get /user/output/ /home/hadoop_tp/

4. Shutting Down the HDFS

You can shut down the HDFS by using the following command.

$ stop-dfs.sh

There are many more commands in **"$HADOOP_HOME/bin/hadoop fs"** than are demonstrated here, although these basic operations will get you started. Running ./bin/hadoop dfs with no additional arguments will list all the commands that can be run with the FsShell system. Furthermore, **$HADOOP_HOME/bin/hadoop fs -help** commandName will display a short usage summary for the operation in question, if you are stuck.

A table of all the operations is shown below. The following conventions are used for parameters

"<path>" means any file or directory name.
"<path>..." means one or more file or directory names.
"<file>" means any filename.
"<src>" and "<dest>" are path names in a directed operation.
"<localSrc>" and "<localDest>" are paths as above, but on the local file system.

All other files and path names refer to the objects inside HDFS.

Sr.No	Command & Description
1	**-ls <path>** Lists the contents of the directory specified by path, showing the names, permissions, owner, size and modification date for each entry.
2	**-lsr <path>** Behaves like -ls, but recursively displays entries in all subdirectories of path.
3	**-du <path>** Shows disk usage, in bytes, for all the files which match path; filenames are reported with the full HDFS protocol prefix.
4	**-dus <path>** Like -du, but prints a summary of disk usage of all files/directories in the path.
5	**-mv <src><dest>** Moves the file or directory indicated by src to dest, within HDFS.
6	**-cp <src> <dest>** Copies the file or directory identified by src to dest, within HDFS.

7	**-rm <path>** Removes the file or empty directory identified by path.
8	**-rmr <path>** Removes the file or directory identified by path. Recursively deletes any child entries (i.e., files or subdirectories of path).
9	**-put <localSrc> <dest>** Copies the file or directory from the local file system identified by localSrc to dest within the DFS.
10	**-copyFromLocal <localSrc> <dest>** Identical to -put
11	**-moveFromLocal <localSrc> <dest>** Copies the file or directory from the local file system identified by localSrc to dest within HDFS, and then deletes the local copy on success.
12	**-get [-crc] <src> <localDest>** Copies the file or directory in HDFS identified by src to the local file system path identified by localDest.
13	**-getmerge <src> <localDest>** Retrieves all files that match the path src in HDFS, and copies them to a single, merged file in the local file system identified by localDest.
14	**-cat <filen-ame>** Displays the contents of filename on stdout.
15	**-copyToLocal <src> <localDest>** Identical to -get
16	**-moveToLocal <src> <localDest>** Works like -get, but deletes the HDFS copy on success.
17	**-mkdir <path>** Creates a directory named path in HDFS.

	Creates any parent directories in path that are missing (e.g., mkdir -p in Linux).
18	**-setrep [-R] [-w] rep <path>** Sets the target replication factor for files identified by path to rep. (The actual replication factor will move toward the target over time)
19	**-touchz <path>** Creates a file at path containing the current time as a timestamp. Fails if a file already exists at path, unless the file is already size 0.
20	**-test -[ezd] <path>** Returns 1 if path exists; has zero length; or is a directory or 0 otherwise.
21	**-stat [format] <path>** Prints information about path. Format is a string which accepts file size in blocks (%b), filename (%n), block size (%o), replication (%r), and modification date (%y, %Y).
22	**-tail [-f] <file2name>** Shows the last 1KB of file on stdout.
23	**-chmod [-R] mode,mode,... <path>...** Changes the file permissions associated with one or more objects identified by path.... Performs changes recursively with R. mode is a 3-digit octal mode, or {augo}+/-{rwxX}. Assumes if no scope is specified and does not apply an umask.
24	**-chown [-R] [owner][:[group]] <path>...** Sets the owning user and/or group for files or directories identified by path.... Sets owner recursively if -R is specified.
25	**-chgrp [-R] group <path>...** Sets the owning group for files or directories identified by path.... Sets group recursively if -R is specified.

26	**-help <cmd-name>** Returns usage information for one of the commands listed above. You must omit the leading '-' character in cmd

As the whole cluster cannot be demonstrated, we are explaining the Hadoop cluster environment using three systems (one master and two slaves); given below are their IP addresses.

- Hadoop Master: 192.168.1.15 (hadoop-master)
- Hadoop Slave: 192.168.1.16 (hadoop-slave-1)
- Hadoop Slave: 192.168.1.17 (hadoop-slave-2)

Follow the steps given below to have Hadoop Multi-Node cluster setup.

5. Installing Java

Java is the main prerequisite for Hadoop. First of all, you should verify the existence of java in your system using "java -version". The syntax of java version command is given below.

$ java -version

If everything works fine it will give you the following output.

java version "1.7.0_71"
Java(TM) SE Runtime Environment (build 1.7.0_71-b13)
Java HotSpot(TM) Client VM (build 25.0-b02, mixed mode)

If java is not installed in your system, then follow the given steps for installing java.

Step 1

Download java (JDK <latest version> - X64.tar.gz) by visiting the following link www.oracle.com

Then **jdk-7u71-linux-x64.tar.gz** will be downloaded into your system.

Step 2

Generally, you will find the downloaded java file in Downloads folder. Verify it and extract the **jdk-7u71-linux-x64.gz** file using the following commands.

```
$ cd Downloads/
$ ls
jdk-7u71-Linux-x64.gz
$ tar zxf jdk-7u71-Linux-x64.gz
$ ls
jdk1.7.0_71 jdk-7u71-Linux-x64.gz
```

Step 3

To make java available to all the users, you have to move it to the location "/usr/local/". Open the root, and type the following commands.

```
$ su
password:
# mv jdk1.7.0_71 /usr/local/
# exit
```

Step 4

For setting up **PATH** and **JAVA_HOME** variables, add the following commands to **~/.bashrc** file.

```
export JAVA_HOME=/usr/local/jdk1.7.0_71
export PATH=PATH:$JAVA_HOME/bin
```

Now verify the **java -version** command from the terminal as explained above. Follow the above process and install java in all your cluster nodes.

6. Creating User Account

Create a system user account on both master and slave systems to use the Hadoop installation.

```
# useradd hadoop
```

passwd hadoop

7. Mapping the nodes

You have to edit **hosts** file in **/etc/** folder on all nodes, specify the IP address of each system followed by their host names.

vi /etc/hosts

enter the following lines in the /etc/hosts file.
192.168.1.109 hadoop-master
192.168.1.145 hadoop-slave-1
192.168.56.1hadoop-slave-2

8. Configuring Key Based Login

Setup ssh in every node such that they can communicate with one another without any prompt for password.

# su hadoop
$ ssh-keygen -t rsa
$ ssh-copy-id -i ~/.ssh/id_rsa.pub tutorialspoint@hadoop-master
$ ssh-copy-id -i ~/.ssh/id_rsa.pub hadoop_tp1@hadoop-slave-1
$ ssh-copy-id -i ~/.ssh/id_rsa.pub hadoop_tp2@hadoop-slave-2
$ chmod 0600 ~/.ssh/authorized_keys
$ exit

9. Installing Hadoop
In the Master server, download and install Hadoop using the following commands.

mkdir /opt/hadoop
cd /opt/hadoop/
wget http://apache.mesi.com.ar/hadoop/common/hadoop-1.2.1/hadoop-1.2.0.tar.gz
tar -xzf hadoop-1.2.0.tar.gz
mv hadoop-1.2.0 hadoop
chown -R hadoop /opt/hadoop
cd /opt/hadoop/hadoop/

10. Configuring Hadoop

You have to configure Hadoop server by making the following changes as given below.

core-site.xml

Open the **core-site.xml** file and edit it as shown below.

```
<configuration>
  <property>
    <name>fs.default.name</name>
    <value>hdfs://hadoop-master:9000/</value>
  </property>
  <property>
    <name>dfs.permissions</name>
    <value>false</value>
  </property>
</configuration>
```

hdfs-site.xml

Open the **hdfs-site.xml** file and edit it as shown below.

```
<configuration>
  <property>
    <name>dfs.data.dir</name>
    <value>/opt/hadoop/hadoop/dfs/name/data</value>
    <final>true</final>
  </property>
  <property>
    <name>dfs.name.dir</name>
    <value>/opt/hadoop/hadoop/dfs/name</value>
    <final>true</final>
  </property>
  <property>
    <name>dfs.replication</name>
    <value>1</value>
  </property>
</configuration>
```

mapred-site.xml

Open the **mapred-site.xml** file and edit it as shown below.

```
<configuration>
  <property>
    <name>mapred.job.tracker</name>
    <value>hadoop-master:9001</value>
  </property>
</configuration>
```

hadoop-env.sh

Open the **hadoop-env.sh** file and edit JAVA_HOME, HADOOP_CONF_DIR, and HADOOP_OPTS as shown below.

Note – Set the JAVA_HOME as per your system configuration.

```
export JAVA_HOME=/opt/jdk1.7.0_17
export HADOOP_OPTS=-Djava.net.preferIPv4Stack=true
export HADOOP_CONF_DIR=/opt/hadoop/hadoop/conf
```

11. Installing Hadoop on Slave Servers

Install Hadoop on all the slave servers by following the given commands.

```
# su hadoop
$ cd /opt/hadoop
$ scp -r hadoop hadoop-slave-1:/opt/hadoop
$ scp -r hadoop hadoop-slave-2:/opt/hadoop
```

Configuring Hadoop on Master Server

Open the master server and configure it by following the given commands.

```
# su hadoop
$ cd /opt/hadoop/Hadoop
```

Configuring Master Node

```
$ vi etc/hadoop/masters
hadoop-master
```

Configuring Slave Node

```
$ vi etc/hadoop/slaves
hadoop-slave-1
hadoop-slave-2
```

Format Name Node on Hadoop Master

```
# su hadoop
$ cd /opt/hadoop/hadoop
$ bin/hadoop namenode –format
11/10/14 10:58:07 INFO namenode.NameNode: STARTUP_MSG:
/************************************************************
STARTUP_MSG: Starting NameNode
STARTUP_MSG: host = hadoop-master/192.168.1.109
STARTUP_MSG: args = [-format]
STARTUP_MSG: version = 1.2.0
STARTUP_MSG: build =
https://svn.apache.org/repos/asf/hadoop/common/branches/bra
nch-1.2 -r 1479473;
compiled by 'hortonfo' on Mon May 6 06:59:37 UTC 2013
STARTUP_MSG: java = 1.7.0_71

************************************************************/
11/10/14 10:58:08 INFO util.GSet: Computing capacity for map
BlocksMap
editlog=/opt/hadoop/hadoop/dfs/name/current/edits
……………………………………………….
……………………………………………….
……………………………………………….
11/10/14 10:58:08 INFO common.Storage: Storage directory
/opt/hadoop/hadoop/dfs/name has been successfully formatted.
11/10/14 10:58:08 INFO namenode.NameNode:
SHUTDOWN_MSG:
/************************************************************
```

SHUTDOWN_MSG: Shutting down NameNode at hadoop-master/192.168.1.15
**/

4.8 Starting Hadoop Services

The following command is to start all the Hadoop services on the Hadoop-Master.

```
$ cd $HADOOP_HOME/sbin
$ start-all.sh
```

1. Adding a New DataNode in the Hadoop Cluster

Given below are the steps to be followed for adding new nodes to a Hadoop cluster.

Networking

Add new nodes to an existing Hadoop cluster with some appropriate network configuration. Assume the following network configuration.

For New node Configuration
IP address : 192.168.1.103
netmask : 255.255.255.0
hostname : slave3.in

2. Adding User and SSH Access

Add a User: On a new node, add "hadoop" user and set password of Hadoop user to "hadoop123" or anything you want by using the following commands.

```
useradd hadoop
passwd hadoop
```

Setup Password less connectivity from master to new slave.

3. Execute the following on the master

```
mkdir -p $HOME/.ssh
```

chmod 700 $HOME/.ssh
ssh-keygen -t rsa -P '' -f $HOME/.ssh/id_rsa
cat $HOME/.ssh/id_rsa.pub >> $HOME/.ssh/authorized_keys
chmod 644 $HOME/.ssh/authorized_keys
Copy the public key to new slave node in hadoop user $HOME directory
scp $HOME/.ssh/id_rsa.pub hadoop@192.168.1.103:/home/hadoop/

4. Execute the following on the slaves

Login to hadoop. If not, login to hadoop user.
su hadoop ssh -X hadoop@192.168.1.103

Copy the content of public key into file **"$HOME/.ssh/authorized_keys"** and then change the permission for the same by executing the following commands.

cd $HOME
mkdir -p $HOME/.ssh
chmod 700 $HOME/.ssh
cat id_rsa.pub >>$HOME/.ssh/authorized_keys
chmod 644 $HOME/.ssh/authorized_keys

Check ssh login from the master machine. Now check if you can ssh to the new node without a password from the master.
ssh hadoop@192.168.1.103 or hadoop@slave3

5. Set Hostname of New Node

You can set hostname in file **/etc/sysconfig/network**
On new slave3 machine
NETWORKING = yes
HOSTNAME = slave3.in

To make the changes effective, either restart the machine or run hostname command to a new machine with the respective hostname (restart is a good option).

On slave3 node machine –
hostname slave3.in

Update **/etc/hosts** on all machines of the cluster with the following lines –
192.168.1.102 slave3.in slave3

Now try to ping the machine with hostnames to check whether it is resolving to IP or not.

On new node machine –
ping master.in

6. Start the DataNode on New Node

Start the datanode daemon manually using **$HADOOP_HOME/bin/hadoop-daemon.sh script**. It will automatically contact the master (NameNode) and join the cluster. We should also add the new node to the conf/slaves file in the master server. The script-based commands will recognize the new node.

Login to new node

su hadoop or ssh -X hadoop@192.168.1.103

Start HDFS on a newly added slave node by using the following command

./bin/hadoop-daemon.sh start datanode

Check the output of jps command on a new node. It looks as follows.

$ jps
7141 DataNode
10312 Jps

7. Removing a DataNode from the Hadoop Cluster

We can remove a node from a cluster on the fly, while it is running, without any data loss. HDFS provides a decommissioning feature, which ensures that removing a node is performed safely. To use it, follow the steps as given below –

Step 1 – Login to master

Login to master machine user where Hadoop is installed.

```
$ su hadoop
```

Step 2 – Change cluster configuration

An exclude file must be configured before starting the cluster. Add a key named dfs.hosts.exclude to our **$HADOOP_HOME/etc/hadoop/hdfs-site.xml** file. The value associated with this key provides the full path to a file on the NameNode's local file system which contains a list of machines which are not permitted to connect to HDFS.

For example, add these lines to **etc/hadoop/hdfs-site.xml** file.

```
<property>
  <name>dfs.hosts.exclude</name>
  <value>/home/hadoop/hadoop-1.2.1/hdfs_exclude.txt</value>
  <description>DFS exclude</description>
</property>
```

Step 3 – Determine hosts to decommission

Each machine to be decommissioned should be added to the file identified by the hdfs_exclude.txt, one domain name per line. This will prevent them from connecting to the NameNode. Content of the **"/home/hadoop/hadoop-1.2.1/hdfs_exclude.txt"** file is shown below, if you want to remove DataNode2.

```
slave2.in
```

Step 4 – Force configuration reload

Run the command **"$HADOOP_HOME/bin/hadoop dfsadmin -refreshNodes"** without the quotes.

```
$ $HADOOP_HOME/bin/hadoop dfsadmin -refreshNodes
```

This will force the NameNode to re-read its configuration, including the newly updated 'excludes' file. It will decommission the nodes over a period of time, allowing time for each node's blocks to be replicated onto machines which are scheduled to remain active.

On **slave2.in**, check the jps command output. After some time, you will see the DataNode process is shutdown automatically.

Step 5 – Shutdown nodes

After the decommission process has been completed, the decommissioned hardware can be safely shut down for maintenance. Run the report command to dfsadmin to check the status of decommission. The following command will describe the status of the decommission node and the connected nodes to the cluster.
$ $HADOOP_HOME/bin/hadoop dfsadmin -report

Step 6 – Edit excludes file again

Once the machines have been decommissioned, they can be removed from the 'excludes' file. Running **"$HADOOP_HOME/bin/hadoop dfsadmin -refreshNodes"** again will read the excludes file back into the NameNode; allowing the DataNodes to rejoin the cluster after the maintenance has been completed, or additional capacity is needed in the cluster again, etc.

Special Note – If the above process is followed and the tasktracker process is still running on the node, it needs to be shut down. One way is to disconnect the machine as we did in the above steps. The Master will recognize the process automatically and will declare as dead. There is no need to follow the same process for removing the tasktracker because it is NOT much crucial as compared to the DataNode. DataNode contains the data that you want to remove safely without any loss of data.

The tasktracker can be run/shutdown on the fly by the following command at any point of time.

```
$ $HADOOP_HOME/bin/hadoop-daemon.sh stop tasktracker
$HADOOP_HOME/bin/hadoop-daemon.sh start tasktracker
```

4.9 HDFC Daemons

HDFS is a **Userspace File System**. Traditionally file systems are embedded in the operating system kernel and runs as an operating system process. But HDFS is not embedded in the operating system kernel. It runs as a User process within the process space allocated for user processes, on the operating system process table. On a traditional process system, the block size is of **4-8KB** whereas in HDFS the default block size is of 64MB.

- HDFS <- GFS
- Userspace File System
- Default Block Size = 64 MB

HDFS is Hadoop Distributed File System, which is responsible for storing data on the cluster in Hadoop. Files in HDFS are split into blocks before they are stored on the cluster. The typical size of a block is 64MB or 128MB. The blocks belonging to one file are then stored on different nodes. The blocks are also replicated to ensure high reliability. To delve deeper into how HDFS achieves all this, we need to first understand **Hadoop Daemons**.

Daemons in computing terms is a process that runs in the background. Hadoop has five such daemons.

1. NameNode
2. Secondary NameNode
3. DataNode
4. JobTracker
5. TaskTracker.

Each daemon runs separately in its own JVM.

1. Namenode

The **namenode** daemon is a master daemon and is responsible for storing all the location information of the files present in HDFS. The actual data is never stored on a namenode. In other words, it holds the metadata of the files in HDFS.

The namenode maintains the entire metadata in RAM, which helps clients receive quick responses to read requests. Therefore, it is important to run namenode from a machine that has lots of RAM at its disposal. The higher the number of files in HDFS, the higher the consumption of RAM. The namenode daemon also maintains a persistent checkpoint of the metadata in a file stored on the disk called the fsimage file.

Whenever a file is placed/deleted/updated in the cluster, an entry of this action is updated in a file called the edits logfile. After updating the edits log, the metadata present in-memory is also updated accordingly. It is important to note that the fsimage file is not updated for every write operation.

In case the namenode daemon is restarted, the following sequence of events occur at namenode boot up,

1. Read the fsimage file from the disk and load it into memory (RAM).
2. Read the actions that are present in the edits log and apply each action to the in-memory representation of the fsimage file.
3. Write the modified in-memory representation to the fsimage file on the disk.

The preceding steps make sure that the in-memory representation is up to date.

The namenode daemon is a single point of failure in Hadoop 1.x, which means that if the node hosting the namenode daemon fails, the filesystem becomes unusable. To handle this, the administrator has to configure the namenode to write the fsimage file to the local disk as well as a remote disk on the network. This backup on the remote disk can be used to restore the namenode on a freshly installed server. Newer versions of Apache Hadoop (2.x) now support **High Availability** (**HA**), which deploys two namenodes in an active/passive configuration, wherein if the active namenode fails, the control falls onto the passive namenode, making it active. This configuration reduces the downtime in case of a namenode failure. As the fsimage file is not updated for every operation, it is possible the edits logfile would grow to a very large file. The restart of namenode service would become very slow because all the actions in the large edits logfile will have to be applied on the fsimage file. The slow boot up time could be avoided using the secondary namenode daemon.

2. Secondary namenode

The **secondary namenode** daemon is responsible for performing periodic housekeeping functions for namenode. It only creates checkpoints of the filesystem metadata (fsimage) present in namenode by merging the edits logfile and the fsimage file from the namenode daemon. In case the namenode daemon fails, this checkpoint could be used to rebuild the filesystem metadata.

However, it is important to note that checkpoints are done in intervals and it is possible that the checkpoint data could be slightly outdated. Rebuilding the fsimage file using such a checkpoint could lead to data loss. The secondary namenode is not a failover node for the namenode daemon.

It is recommended that the secondary namenode daemon be hosted on a separate machine for large clusters. The checkpoints are created by merging the edits logfiles and the fsimage file from the namenode daemon.

The following are the steps carried out by the secondary namenode daemon

1. Get the edits logfile from the primary namenode daemon.
2. Get the fsimage file from the primary namenode daemon.
3. Apply all the actions present in the edits logs to the fsimage file.
4. Push the fsimage file back to the primary namenode.

This is done periodically and so whenever the namenode daemon is restarted, it would have a relatively updated version of the

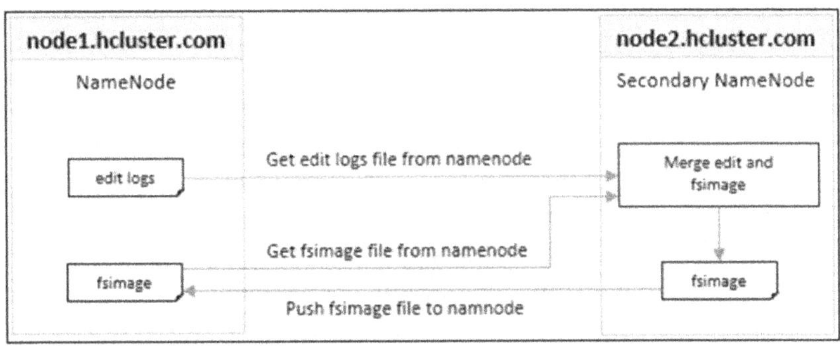

fsimage file and the boot up time would be significantly faster. The following diagram shows the communication between namenode and secondary namenode.

3. Datanode

The **datanode** daemon acts as a slave node and is responsible for storing the actual files in HDFS. The files are split as data blocks across the cluster. The blocks are typically 64 MB to 128 MB size blocks. The block size is a configurable parameter. The file blocks in a Hadoop cluster also replicate themselves to other datanodes for redundancy so that no data is lost in case a datanode daemon fails. The datanode daemon sends information to the namenode daemon about the files and blocks stored in that node and responds to the namenode daemon for all filesystem operations. The following diagram shows how files are stored in the cluster.

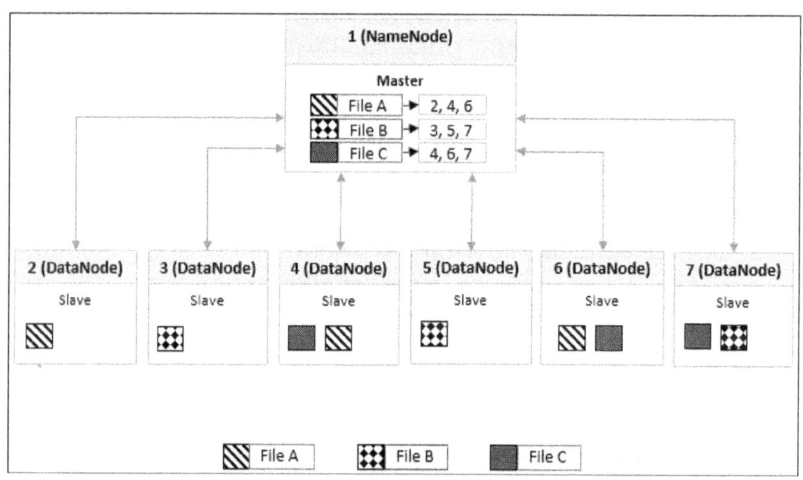

File blocks of files A, B, and C are replicated across multiple nodes of the cluster for redundancy. This ensures availability of data even if one of the nodes fail. You can also see that blocks of file A are present on nodes 2, 4, and 6; blocks of file B are present on nodes 3, 5, and 7; and blocks of file C are present on 4, 6, and 7.

The replication factor configured for this cluster is 3, which signifies that each file block is replicated three times across the cluster. It is the responsibility of the namenode daemon to maintain a list of the files and their corresponding locations on the cluster. Whenever a client needs to access a file, the namenode daemon provides the location of the file to client and the client, then accesses the file directly from the datanode daemon.

4. Jobtracker

The **jobtracker** daemon is responsible for accepting job requests from a client and scheduling/assigning tasktrackers with tasks to be performed. The jobtracker daemon tries to assign tasks to the tasktracker daemon on the datanode daemon where the data to be processed is stored. This feature is called **data locality**. If that is not possible, it will at least try to assign tasks to tasktrackers within the same physical server rack. If for some reason the node hosting the datanode and tasktracker daemons fails, the jobtracker daemon assigns the task to another tasktracker daemon where the replica of the data exists. This is possible because of the replication factor configuration for HDFS where the data blocks are replicated across multiple datanodes. This ensures that the job does not fail even if a node fails within the cluster.

5. Tasktracker

The **tasktracker** daemon is a daemon that accepts tasks (map, reduce, and shuffle) from the jobtracker daemon. The tasktracker daemon is the daemon that performs the actual tasks during a MapReduce operation. The tasktracker daemon sends a heartbeat message to jobtracker, periodically, to notify the jobtracker daemon that it is alive. Along with the heartbeat, it also sends the free slots available within it, to process tasks. The tasktracker daemon starts and monitors the map and reduces tasks and sends progress/status information back to the jobtracker daemon.

In small clusters, the namenode and jobtracker daemons reside on the same node. However, in larger clusters, there are dedicated nodes for the namenode and jobtracker daemons. This can be easily understood from the following diagram:

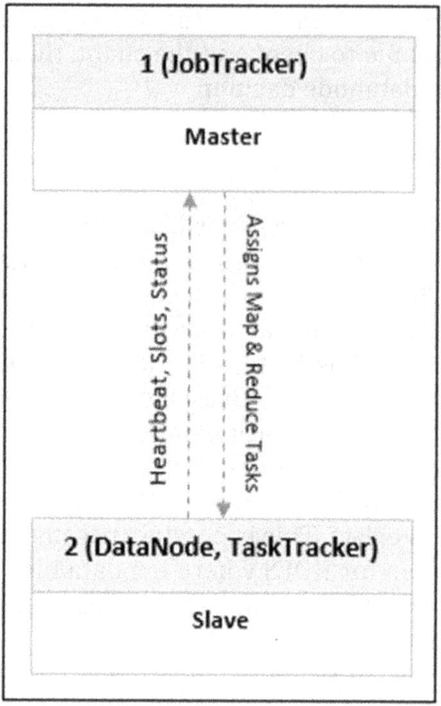

In a Hadoop cluster, these daemons can be monitored via specific URLs using a browser. The specific URLs are of the http://<serveraddress>:port_number type.

By default, the ports for the Hadoop daemons are:

The Hadoop daemon	Port
Namenode	50070
Secondary namenode	50090
Jobtracker	50030
Datanode	50075
Tasktracker	50060

4.10 Hadoop HDFS Data Read and Write Operations

HDFS follow *Write once Read many* models. So, we cannot edit files already stored in HDFS, but we can append data by reopening the file. In Read-Write operation client first, interact with the NameNode.

NameNode provides privileges so, the client can easily read and write data blocks into/from the respective datanodes. In this blog, we will discuss the internals of Hadoop HDFS data read and write operations. We will also cover how client read and write the data from HDFS, how the client interacts with master and slave nodes in HDFS data read and write operations.

HDFS – *Hadoop Distributed File System* is the storage layer of Hadoop. It is most reliable storage system on the planet. HDFS works in *master-slave* fashion, NameNode is the master daemon which runs on the master node, DataNode is the slave daemon which runs on the slave node.

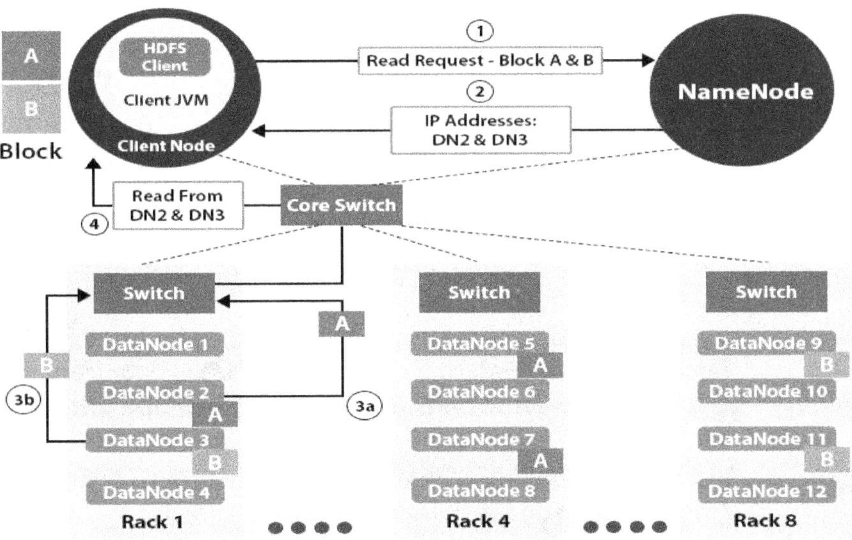

4.10.1 HDFS Read Operation

Suppose the HDFS client wants to read a file "File.txt". Let the file be divided into two blocks say, A and B. The following steps will take place during the file read.

1. The Client interacts with HDFS NameNode

a) As the NameNode stores the block's metadata for the file "File.txt', the client will reach out to NameNode asking locations of DataNodes containing data blocks.
b) The NameNode first checks for required privileges, and if the client has sufficient privileges, the NameNode sends the locations of DataNodes containing blocks (A and B). NameNode also gives a **security token** to the client, which they need to show to the DataNodes for authentication. Let the NameNode provide the following list of IPs for block A and B – for block A, location of DataNodes D2, D5, D7, and for block B, location of DataNodes D3, D9, D11.

To perform various **HDFS operations** (read, write, copy, move, change permission, etc.) follow **HDFS command list**.

2. The client interacts with HDFS DataNode

a) After receiving the addresses of the DataNodes, the client directly interacts with the DataNodes. The client will send a request to the closest DataNodes (D2 for block A and D3 for block B) through the **FSDataInputstream** object. The **DFSInputstream** manages the interaction between client and DataNode.
b) The client will show the security tokens provided by NameNode to the DataNodes and start reading data from the DataNode. The data will flow directly from the DataNode to the client.
c) After reading all the required file blocks, the client calls close() method on the FSDataInputStream object.

Now let us see how internally read operation is carried out in Hadoop HDFS, how data flows between the client, the NameNode, and DataNodes during file read.

3. Internals of file read in HDFS

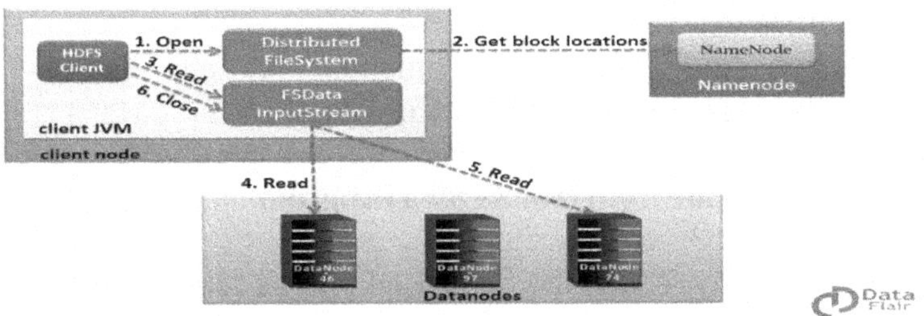

1. In order to open the required file, the client calls the **open()** method on the **FileSystem object**, which for HDFS is an instance of DistributedFilesystem.
2. DistributedFileSystem then calls the NameNode using RPC to get the locations of the first few blocks of a file. For each **data block**, NameNode returns the addresses of Datanodes that contain a copy of that block. Furthermore, the DataNodes are sorted based on their proximity to the client.
3. The DistributedFileSystem returns an **FSDataInputStream** to the client from where the client can read the data. FSDataInputStream in succession wraps a DFSInputStream. **DFSInputStream** manages the I/O of DataNode and NameNode.
4. Then the client calls the **read()** method on the **FSDataInputStream** object.
5. The DFSInputStream, which contains the addresses for the first few blocks in the file, connects to the closest DataNode to read the first block in the file. Then, the data flows from DataNode to the client, which calls read() repeatedly on the FSDataInputStream.
6. Upon reaching the end of the file, DFSInputStream closes the connection with that DataNode and finds the best suited DataNode for the next block.
7. If the DFSInputStream during reading, faces an error while communicating with a DataNode, it will try the other closest DataNode for that block. DFSInputStream will also remember DataNodes that have failed so that it doesn't needlessly retry them for later blocks. Also, the DFSInputStream veri-

fies checksums for the data transferred to it from the DataNode. If it finds any corrupt block, it reports this to the NameNode and reads a copy of the block from another DataNode.

8. When the client has finished reading the data, it calls **close()** on the **FSDataInputStream**.

4. How to Read a file from HDFS – Java Program

A sample code to read a file from HDFS is as follows (To perform HDFS read and write operations:

```
FileSystem fileSystem = FileSystem.get(conf);
Path path = new Path("/path/to/file.ext");
if (!fileSystem.exists(path)) {
System.out.println("File does not exists");
return;
}
FSDataInputStream in = fileSystem.open(path);
int numBytes = 0;
while ((numBytes = in.read(b))> 0) {
System.out.prinln((char)numBytes));// code to manipulate the data which is read
}
in.close();
out.close();
```

4.10.2 HDFS Write Operation

To write data in HDFS, the client first interacts with the **NameNode** to get permission to write data and to get IPs of **DataNodes** where the client writes the data. The client then directly interacts with the DataNodes for writing data. The DataNode then creates a replica of the data block to other DataNodes in the pipeline based on the replication factor.

DFSOutputStream in HDFS maintains two queues (data queue and ack queue) during the write operation.

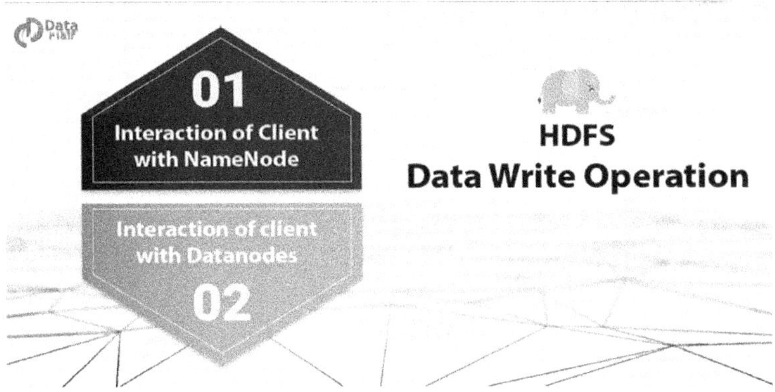

1. The client interacts with HDFS NameNode

a) To write a file inside the HDFS, the client first interacts with the NameNode. NameNode first checks for the client privileges to write a file. If the client has sufficient privilege and there is no file existing with the same name, NameNode then creates a record of a new file.
b) NameNode then provides the address of all DataNodes, where the client can write its data. It also provides a security token to the client, which they need to present to the DataNodes before writing the block.
c) If the file already exists in the HDFS, then file creation fails, and the client receives an **IO Exception**.

2. The client interacts with HDFS DataNode

After receiving the list of the DataNodes and file write permission, the client starts writing data directly to the first DataNode in the list. As the client finishes writing data to the first DataNode, the DataNode starts making replicas of a block to other DataNodes depending on the replication factor.

If the replication factor is 3, then there will be a minimum of 3 copies of blocks created in different DataNodes, and after creating required replicas, it sends an acknowledgment to the client.

3. Internals of file write in Hadoop HDFS

Let us understand the HDFS write operation in detail. The following steps will take place while writing a file to the HDFS,

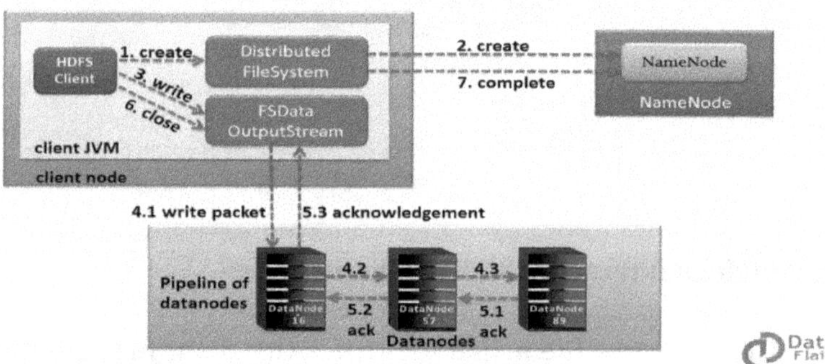

1. The client calls the **create()** method on **DistributedFileSystem** to create a file.
2. DistributedFileSystem interacts with NameNode through the RPC call to create a new file in the filesystem namespace with no blocks associated with it.
3. The NameNode checks for the client privileges and makes sure that the file doesn't already exist. If the client has sufficient privileges and no file with the same name exists, the NameNode makes a record of the new file. Otherwise, the client receives an I/O exception, and file creation fails. The DistributedFileSystem then returns an FSDataOutputStream for the client where the client starts writing data. FSDataOutputstream, in turn, wraps a DFSOutputStream, which handles communication with the DataNodes and NameNode.
4. As the client starts writing data, the **DFSOutputStream** splits the client's data into packets and writes it to an internal queue called the **data queue**. **DataStreamer**, which is responsible for telling the NameNode to allocate new blocks by choosing the list of suitable DataNode to store the replicas, uses this data queue. The list of DataNode forms a pipeline. The number of DataNodes in the pipeline depends on the replication factor. Suppose the replication factor is 3, so

there are three nodes in the pipeline.The DataStreamer streams the packet to the first DataNode in the pipeline, which stores each packet and forwards it to the second node in the pipeline. Similarly, the second DataNode stores the packet and transfers it to the next node in the pipeline (last node).

5. The **DFSOutputStream** also maintains another queue of packets, called **ack queue,** which is waiting for the acknowledgment from DataNodes. Packet in the ack queue gets remove only when it receives an acknowledgment from all the DataNodes in the pipeline.
6. The client calls the **close()** method on the stream when he/she finishes writing data. Thus, before communicating the NameNode to signal about the file complete, the client close() method's action pushes the remaining packets to the DataNode pipeline and waits for the acknowledgment.
7. As the Namenode already knows about the blocks (the file made of), so the NameNode only waits for blocks to be minimally replicated before returning successfully.

4. What happens if DataNode fails while writing a file in the HDFS?

While writing data to the DataNode, if DataNode fails, then the following actions take place, which is transparent to the client writing the data.

1. The pipeline gets closed, packets in the ack queue are then added to the front of the data queue making DataNodes downstream from the failed node to not miss any packet.
2. Then the current block on the alive DataNode gets a new identity. This id is then communicated to the NameNode so that, later on, if the failed DataNode recovers, the partial block on the failed DataNode will be deleted.
3. The failed DataNode gets removed from the pipeline, and a new pipeline gets constructed from the two alive DataNodes. The remaining of the block's data is then written to the alive DataNodes, added in the pipeline.
4. The NameNode observes that the block is **under-replicated**, and it arranges for creating further copy on another DataNode. Other coming blocks are then treated as normal.

5. How to Write a file in HDFS – Java Program

A sample code to write a file to HDFS in Java is as follows:

```
FileSystem fileSystem = FileSystem.get(conf);
// Check if the file already exists
Path path = new Path("/path/to/file.ext");
if (fileSystem.exists(path)) {
System.out.println("File " + dest + " already exists");
return;
}
// Create a new file and write data to it.
FSDataOutputStream out = fileSystem.create(path);
InputStream in = new BufferedInputStream(new FileInputStream(
new File(source)));
byte[] b = new byte[1024];
int numBytes = 0;
while ((numBytes = in.read(b)) > 0) {
out.write(b, 0, numBytes);
}
// Close all the file descripters
in.close();
out.close();
```

4.11 Replica Processing of Data with Hadoop

Hadoop Distributed File System (HDFS) is designed to store data on inexpensive, and more unreliable, hardware. *Inexpensive* has an attractive ring to it, but it does raise concerns about the reliability of the system as a whole, especially for ensuring the high availability of the data.

Planning ahead for disaster, the brains behind HDFS made the decision to set up the system so that it would store three (count 'em — three) copies of every data block. HDFS assumes that every disk drive and every slave node is inherently unreliable, so, clearly, care must be taken in choosing where the three copies of the data blocks are stored. The figure shows how data blocks from the earlier file are *striped* across the Hadoop cluster — meaning they are evenly distributed between the slave nodes so that a copy of the block will still be available regardless of disk, node, or rack failures.

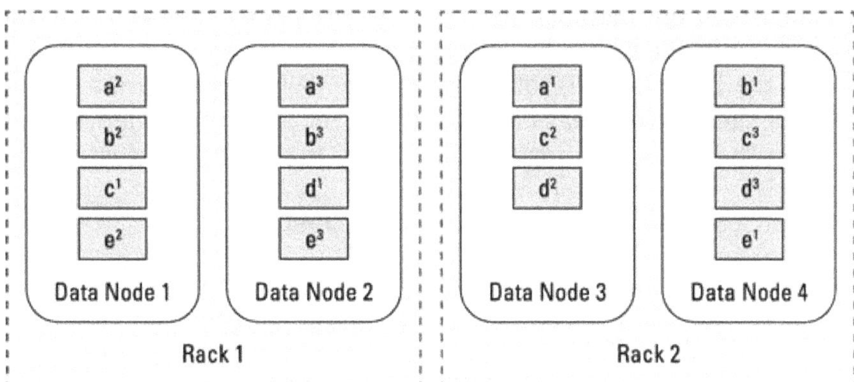

The file shown has five data blocks, labeled a, b, c, d, and e. If you take a closer look, you can see this particular cluster is made up of two racks with two nodes a piece, and that the three copies of each data block have been spread out across the various slave nodes. Every component in the Hadoop cluster is seen as a potential failure point, so when HDFS stores the replicas of the original blocks across the Hadoop cluster, it tries to ensure that the block replicas are stored in different failure points.

For example, take a look at Block A. At the time it needed to be stored, Slave Node 3 was chosen, and the first copy of Block A was stored there. For multiple rack systems, HDFS then determines that the remaining two copies of block A need to be stored in a different rack. So, the second copy of block A is stored on Slave Node 1. The final copy can be stored on the same rack as the second copy, but not on the same slave node, so it gets stored on Slave Node 2. Before going ahead, it is important to know basic information like, what is Replication factor, blocks and block size. So, let's get a clear picture of them first.

1. Blocks and Block Size

HDFS is designed to store and process huge amounts of data and data sets. A typical block size used by HDFS is about 64MB. We can also change the block size in Hadoop Cluster. All blocks in a file, except the last block are of the same size. When you store a file in HDFS, the system breaks it down into a set of individual blocks and stores these blocks in various slave nodes in the Hadoop cluster.

2. Block Size Configuration for Entire Cluster:

If you want to set some specific block size for the entire cluster, you need to add a property into hdfs-site.xml as shown below.

```
<property>
<name>dfs.block.size<name>
<value>134217728<value>
<description>Block size<description>
<property>
```

Here, we have set the dfs.block.size as 128MB. This will be applicable for the entire cluster. Changing the dfs.block.size property in hdfs-site.xml will change the default block size for all the files placed into HDFS. Here, changing the block size will not affect the block size of any files already in HDFS. It will only be applicable for those files which will be placed after this setting takes effect.

4.11.1 Replication Factor

The blocks of a file are replicated for fault tolerance. The block size and replication factor are configurable per file. An application can specify the number of replicas of a file. The replication factor can be specified at the time of creation of the file and can be changed later. Files in HDFS are write-once and have strictly one writer at any time.

The replication factor is a property that can be set in the HDFS configuration file. It also allows you to adjust the global replication factor for the entire cluster. For each block stored in HDFS, there will be n – 1 duplicated blocks distributed across the cluster.

Example:

If you want to set 4 as the replication factor for the entire cluster, then you need to specify the replication factor into the **hdfs-site.xml.**

```
<configuration>
<property>
<name>dfs.replication</name>
<value>4</value>            <!-- Here you need to set replication fac-
tor for entire cluster. -->
</property>
<property>
<name>dfs.namenode.name.dir</name>
<value>/home/acadgild/hadoop/namenode</value>
</property>
<property>
<name>dfs.datanode.data.dir</name>
<value>/home/acadgild/hadoop/datanode</value>
</property>
</configuration>
```

We can also change the replication factor on a file. Let's now create a new directory in HDFS root as shown below.

```
hadoop dfs -mkdir /test1/
```

You can verify this using the command-

```
hadoop fs -ls /
```

Now, let's add a file into this directory.

```
hadoop dfs -put /home/acadgild/acadgild  /test1/
```

Next, let's try running the command to change the replication factor of a file in Hadoop cluster. The command to this is as shown below:

```
hadoop fs –setrep –w 5 /test1/acadgild
```

We can also change the replication factor of all the files within a directory by using the below command.

```
hadoop fs –setrep –w 3 -R /test/
```

We now have three files under this test directory. Therefore, it is considering the first file and will replicate other files later on.

Note: *Replication of individual files and directory takes time and it varies on various factor like:*

- Number of replication factor
- Size of files and directory
- Datanode Hardware

So, it's better not to change replication factor for files basis and directory basis unless you need it. Hope this post has been helpful in understanding the steps to configure block size and replication factor in HDFS.

Replication factor is the process of duplicating the data on the different slave machines to achieve high availability processing.Replication is a Backup mechanism or Failover mechanism or Fault tolerant mechanism.

In Hadoop, Replication factor default is 3 times. No need to configure.

Hadoop 1.x :
Replication Factor is 3
Hadoop 2.x:
Replication Factor is also 3.

In Hadoop, Minimum Replication factor is 1 time. It is possible for a single node Hadoop cluster.

In Hadoop, Maximum Replication factor is 512 times.

f 3 minimum replication factor then minimum 3 slave nodes are required.

If the replication factor is 10 then we need 10 slave nodes are required.

Here is simple for the replication factor:

'N' Replication Factor = 'N' Slave Nodes

1. How to configure Replication in Hadoop?

It is configured in the hdfs-site.xml file.

```
/usr/local/hadoop/conf/hdfs-site.xml
<configuration>
<property>
<name> dfs.replication</name>
<value> 5 </value>
</property>
</value>
```

2. Design Rules of Replication In Hadoop:

1. In Hadoop Replication is only applicable to Hadoop Distributed File System (HDFS) but not for Metadata.
2. Keep One Replication per slave node as per design.
3. Replication will only happen on Hadoop slave nodes alone

but not on Hadoop Master node (because the master node is only for metadata management on its own. It will not maintain the data).

4.12 Managing Resources and Applications with Hadoop YARN

Job scheduling and tracking for big data are integral parts of Hadoop MapReduce and can be used to manage resources and applications. The early versions of Hadoop supported a rudimentary job and task tracking system, but as the mix of work supported by Hadoop changed, the scheduler could not keep up. In particular, the old scheduler could not manage non-MapReduce jobs, and it was incapable of optimizing cluster utilization. So a new capability was designed to address these shortcomings and offer more flexibility, efficiency, and performance. YARN stands for "***Yet Another Resource Negotiator***". It was introduced in Hadoop 2.0 to remove the bottleneck on Job Tracker which was present in Hadoop 1.0. YARN was described as a "*Redesigned Resource Manager*" at the time of its launching, but it has now evolved to be known as large-scale distributed operating system used for Big Data processing.

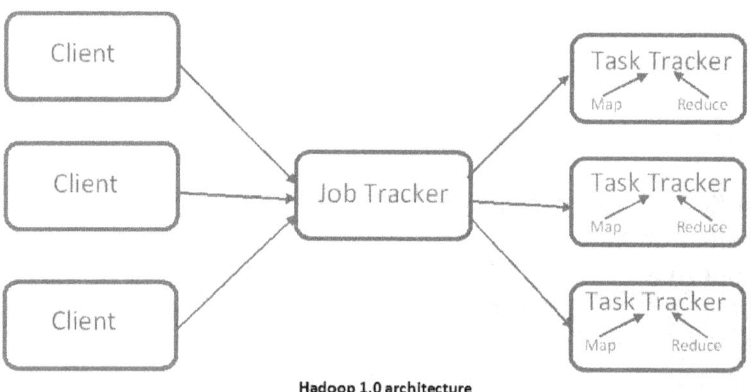

Hadoop 1.0 architecture

Yet Another Resource Negotiator (YARN) is a core Hadoop service providing two major services:

- Global resource management (ResourceManager)
- Per-application management (ApplicationMaster)

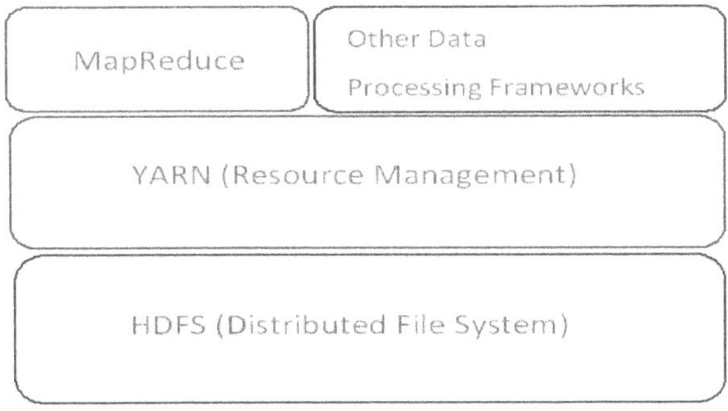

Hadoop 2.0

YARN also allows different data processing engines like graph processing, interactive processing, stream processing as well as batch processing to run and process data stored in HDFS (Hadoop Distributed File System) thus making the system much more efficient. Through its various components, it can dynamically allocate various resources and schedule the application processing. For large volume data processing, it is quite necessary to manage the available resources properly so that every application can leverage them.

YARN Features: YARN gained popularity because of the following features

a) **Scalability:** The scheduler in Resource manager of YARN architecture allows Hadoop to extend and manage thousands of nodes and clusters.
b) **Compatability:** YARN supports the existing map-reduce applications without disruptions thus making it compatible with Hadoop 1.0 as well.
c) **Cluster Utilization:**Since YARN supports Dynamic utilization of cluster in Hadoop, which enables optimized Cluster Utilization.
d) **Multi-tenancy:** It allows multiple engine access thus giving organizations a benefit of multi-tenancy.

4.12.1 Global Resource Management (ResourceManager)

The Resource Manager is the core component of **YARN – Yet Another Resource Negotiator**. In analogy, it occupies the place of JobTracker of MRV1. Hadoop YARN is designed to provide a generic and flexible framework to administer the computing resources in the Hadoop cluster. In this direction, the YARN Resource Manager Service (RM) is the central controlling authority for resource management and makes allocation decisions ResourceManager has two main components: Scheduler and ApplicationsManager.

The **Scheduler** API is specifically designed to negotiate resources and not schedule tasks. The scheduler does not perform monitoring or tracking of status for the Applications. The Scheduler performs its scheduling function based the resource requirements of the applications; it does so base on the abstract notion of a resource Container which incorporates elements such as memory, CPU, disk, network etc.Hadoop Yarn Resource Manager does not guarantee about restarting failed tasks either due to application failure or hardware failures. Applications can request resources at different layers of the cluster topology such as nodes, racks etc. Hence, the scheduler determines how much and where to allocate based on resource availability and the configured sharing policy.The Scheduler has a pluggable policy plug-in, which is responsible for partitioning the cluster resources among the various queues, applications etc.

The current **Map-Reduce** schedulers such as the CapacityScheduler and the FairScheduler would be some examples of the plug-in ApplicationsManager is responsible for maintaining a collection of submitted applications. It accepts a job from the client and negotiates for a container to execute the application specific ApplicationMaster and it provide the service for restarting the ApplicationMaster in the case of failure. It also keeps a cache of completed applications so as to serve users' requests via web UI or command line long after the applications in question finished. Though the above two are the core component, for its complete functionality the Resource Manager depend on various other components.

4.12.2 Hadoop Yarn Resource Manager Components

RM works together with the per-node **NodeManagers** (NMs) and the per-application ApplicationMasters (AMs). The ResourceManager has the following components:

1. Components interfacing RM to the client

a) ClientService: The client interface to the Resource Manager. This component handles all the RPC interfaces to the RM from the clients including operations like application submission, application termination, obtaining queue information, cluster statistics etc.

b) AdminService: To make sure that admin requests don't get starved due to the normal users' requests and to give the operators' commands the higher priority, all the admin operations like refreshing node-list, the queues' configuration etc. are served via this separate interface.

2. Components connecting RM to the nodes

a) ResourceTrackerService: This is the component that obtains heartbeats from nodes in the cluster and forwards them to YarnScheduler. Responds to RPCs from all the nodes, registers new nodes, rejecting requests from any invalid/decommissioned nodes, It works closely with NMLivelinessMonitor and NodesListManager.

b) NMLivelinessMonitor: To keep track of live nodes and dead nodes. This component keeps track of each node's its last heartbeat time. Any node that doesn't send a heartbeat within a configured interval of time, by default 10 minutes, is deemed dead and is expired by the RM. All the containers currently running on an expired node are marked as dead and no new containers are scheduling on such node.

c) NodesListManager: Manages valid and excluded nodes. Responsible for reading the host configuration files and seeding the initial list of nodes based on those files. Keeps track of nodes that are decommissioned as time progresses.

3. Components interacting with the per-application AMs

a) ApplicationMasterService: Services the RPCs from all the AMs like registration of new AMs, termination/unregister-requests from any finishing AMs, obtaining container-allocation & deallocation requests from all running AMs and forward them over to the YarnScheduler. Thus, ApplicationMasterService and AMLivelinessMonitor work together to maintain the fault tolerance of ApplicationMasters.

b) AMLivelinessMonitor: Maintains the list of live AMs and dead/non-responding AMs, Its responsibility is to keep track of live AMs, it usually tracks the AMs dead or alive with the help of heartbeats, and register and de-register the AMs from the Resource manager. Hence, all the containers currently running/allocated to an AM that gets expired are marked as dead.

4. The core of the ResourceManager – the scheduler and related components

a) ApplicationsManager: Responsible for maintaining a collection of submitted applications. Also, keeps a cache of completed applications so as to serve users' requests via web UI or command line long after the applications in question finished.

b) ApplicationACLsManager: RM needs to gate the user facing APIs like the client and admin requests to be accessible only to authorized users. This component maintains the ACLs lists per application and enforces them whenever a request like killing an application, viewing an application status is received.

c) ApplicationMasterLauncher: Maintains a thread-pool to launch AMs of newly submitted applications as well as applications whose previous AM attempts exited due to some reason. Also responsible for cleaning up the AM when an application has finished normally or forcefully terminated.

d) YarnScheduler: Yarn Scheduler is responsible for allocating resources to the various running applications subject to constraints of capacities, queues etc. It also performs its scheduling function based on the resource requirements of the applications. For example, memory, CPU, disk, network etc. Currently, only memory is supported and support for CPU is close to completion.

e) ContainerAllocationExpirer: This component is in charge of ensuring that all allocated containers are used by AMs and subsequently launched on the correspond NMs. AMs run as untrusted user code and can potentially hold on to allocations without using them, and as such can cause cluster under-utilization. To address this, ContainerAllocationExpirer maintains the list of allocated containers that are still not used on the corresponding NMs. For any container, if the corresponding NM doesn't report to the RM that the container has started running within a configured interval of time, by default 10 minutes, then the container is deemed as dead and is expired by the RM.

5. TokenSecretManagers (for security):

Hadoop Yarn Resource Manager has a collection of SecretManagers for the charge/responsibility of managing tokens, secret keys for authenticate/authorize requests on various RPC interfaces. A brief summary follows:

a) ApplicationTokenSecretManager: RM uses the per-application tokens called ApplicationTokens to avoid arbitrary processes from sending RM scheduling requests. This component saves each token locally in memory till application finishes. Then uses it to authenticate any request coming from a valid AM process.

b) ContainerTokenSecretManager: RM issues special tokens called Container Tokens to ApplicationMaster(AM) for a container on the specific node. Hence, these tokens are used by AM to create a connection with NodeManager having the container in which job runs.

c) RMDelegationTokenSecretManager: A ResourceManager specific delegation-token secret-manager. It is responsible for generating delegation tokens to clients which can also be passed on to unauthenticated processes that wish to be able to talk to RM.

6. DelegationTokenRenewer

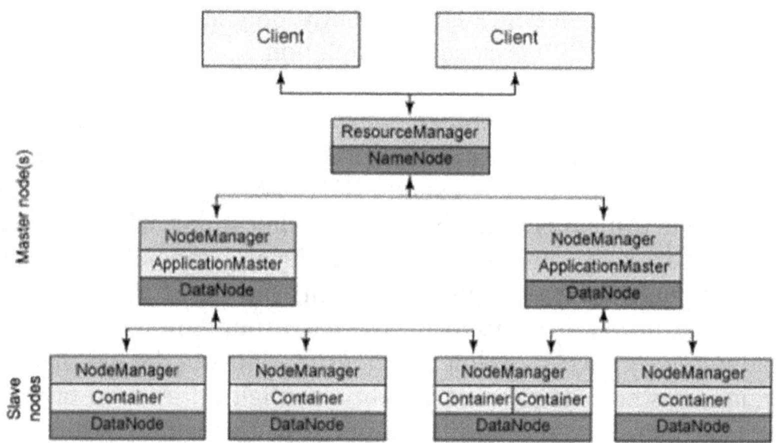

In secure mode, RM is Kerberos authenticated. Hence provides the service of renewing file-system tokens on behalf of the applications. This component renews tokens of submitted applications as long as the application runs and till the tokens can no longer be renewed. The responsibility and functionalities of the NameNode and DataNode remained the same as in MRV1. The below block diagram summarizes the execution flow of job in YARN framework.

7. Per-application management (ApplicationMaster)

Many will draw parallels between YARN and the existing Hadoop MapReduce system (MR1 in Apache Hadoop 1.x). However, the key difference is the *new concept* of an **ApplicationMaster**.

The ApplicationMaster is, in effect, an *instance* of a *framework-specific library* and is responsible for negotiating resources from the ResourceManager and working with the NodeManager(s) to execute and monitor the containers and their resource consumption. It has the responsibility of negotiating appropriate resource containers from the ResourceManager, tracking their status and monitoring progress.

The ApplicationMaster allows YARN to exhibit the following key characteristics:

- **Scale:** The Application Master provides much of the functionality of the traditional ResourceManager so that the entire system can scale more dramatically. In tests, we've already successfully simulated 10,000 node clusters composed of modern hardware without significant issue. This is one of the key reasons that we have chosen to design the ResourceManager as a *pure scheduler* i.e. it doesn't attempt to provide fault-tolerance for resources. We shifted that to become a primary responsibility of the ApplicationMaster instance. Furthermore, since there is an instance of an ApplicationMaster per application, the ApplicationMaster itself isn't a common bottleneck in the cluster.

- **Open:** Moving all application framework specific code into the ApplicationMaster generalizes the system so that we can now support multiple frameworks such as MapReduce, MPI and Graph Processing.

4.12.3 Application Workflow in Hadoop YARN

1. Client submits an application
2. The Resource Manager allocates a container to start the Application Manager
3. The Application Manager registers itself with the Resource Manager
4. The Application Manager negotiates containers from the Resource Manager
5. The Application Manager notifies the Node Manager to launch containers
6. Application code is executed in the container

7. Client contacts Resource Manager/Application Manager to monitor application's status
8. Once the processing is complete, the Application Manager un-registers with the Resource Manager

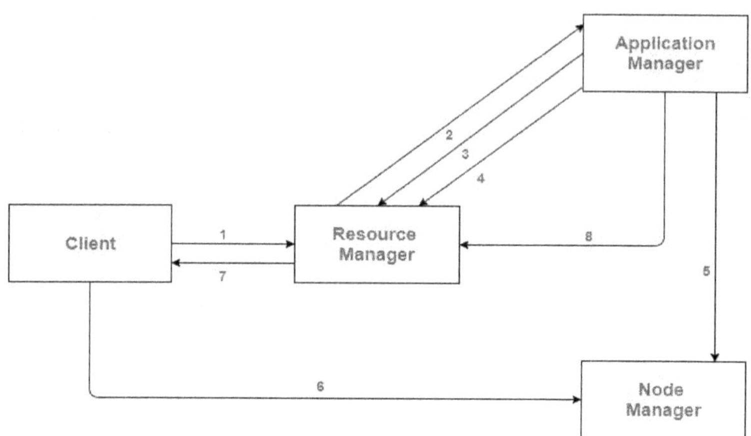

UNIT 5

SOCIAL MEDIA ANALYTICS AND TEXT MINING

The past few years have seen social media mature as a means of communication. From the early days of experimentation and tentative investment by businesses, the primary platforms of social media have evolved, which means that most businesses today will have experimented with using social media, meaning that the process of moving forward is as much about reflection as it is about learning from others. Whether you have social media experience from personal or business use, it is worth thinking about how it works for you now: what engages you, and where are the opportunities.

Without big data analytics, companies are blind and deaf, wandering out onto the web like deer on a freeway
Geoffrey Moore

5.1 Introduction

Knowing how to build appropriate strategies around the key social platforms and implement and monitor them, can provide small and medium-sized firms with a highly cost-effective way of communicating, developing business, undertaking vital research, keeping up to date with the latest developments in their field and creating value for their clients. Social media refers to the means of interactions among people in which they create, share, and/or exchange information and ideas in virtual communities and networks. The Office of Communications and Marketing manages the main Facebook, Twitter, Instagram, Snapchat, YouTube and Vimeo accounts. We offer an array of tools, including one-on-one consults with schools, departments and offices looking to form or maintain an existing social media presence to discuss social media goals and strategy, as well as offer insights and ideas. Before creating any social media account, you must submit the Account Request Form. Be sure to check with your school's communications office for any school specific regulations or branding guidelines.

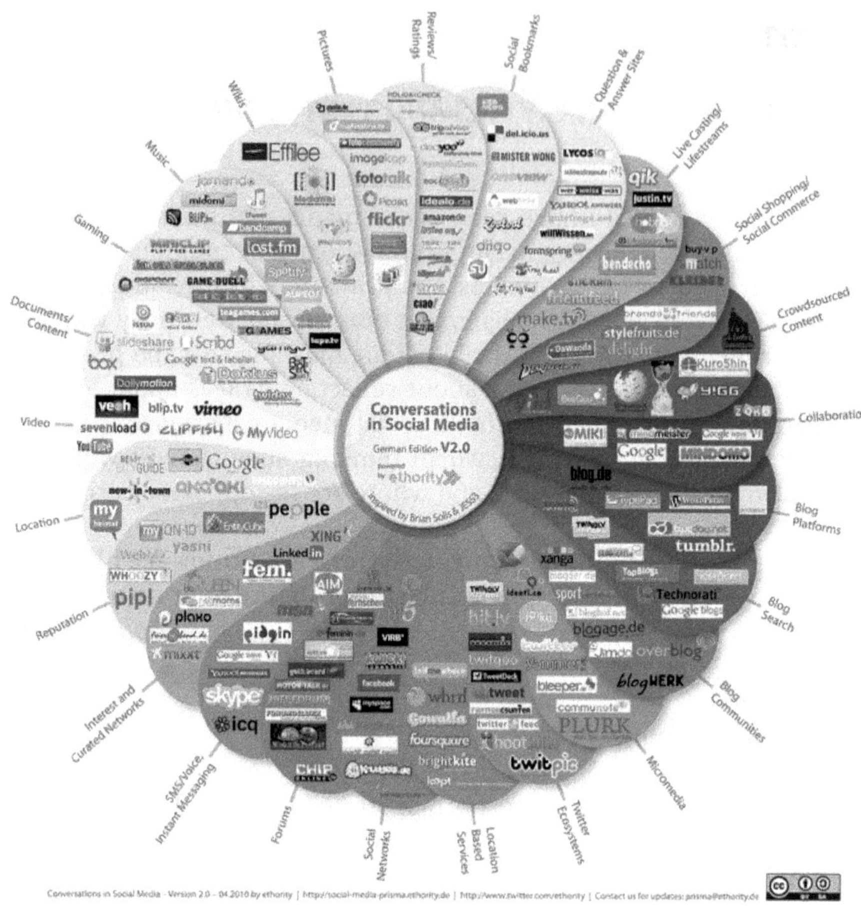

5.1.1 Characteristics of Social Media

Before the term Web 2.0 was coined in 1999, Internet pages featured mostly static content such as text and graphics. Websites operated on Web 1.0 technologies, where website hosts and owners were the primary content contributors. Online information targeted a mostly passive audience that received rather than contributed content. However, with the introduction of Web 2.0 Internet technologies around the turn of the 21st century, social media venues such as blogs began to allow users to interact and collaborate with each other in virtual communities. This more open, communal method of social media dialogue contrasted significantly with the top-down approach that characterized the early years of the web.

Specifically, social media began meeting the characteristics of Web 2.0 websites, providing a rich user experience, dynamic content, scalability, openness and collective intelligence. Active social media users could take advantage of various features that allowed them to 'like,' create and post images, and upload videos and text. Users could then share this information, either with a select group of friends or publicly across the web. However, this has also opened up social media websites to spamming, trolling and flaming by unscrupulous or less mature users. Nevertheless, social media has grown rapidly in the U.S. and around the world due to its blending of technology and social interaction for the co-creation of value.

Key Principles for Social Media Managers

1. Social media is about conversations, community, connecting with the audience and building relationships. It is not just a broadcast channel or a sales and marketing tool.
2. Authenticity, honesty and open dialogue are key.
3. Social media not only allows you to hear what people say about you, but enables you to respond. Listen first, speak second.
4. Be compelling, useful, relevant and engaging. Don't be afraid to try new things, but think through your efforts before kicking them off.

5.1.2 Popular Social Media Tools and Platforms

1. **Blogs:** A platform for casual dialogue and discussions on a specific topic or opinion.
2. **Facebook:** The world's largest social network, with more than 1.55 billion monthly active users (as of the third quarter of 2015). Users create a personal profile, add other users as friends, and exchange messages, including status updates. Brands create pages and Facebook users can "like" brands' pages.
3. **Twitter:** A social networking/micro-blogging platform that allows groups and individuals to stay connected through the exchange of short status messages (140 character limit).
4. **YouTube & Vimeo:** Video hosting and watching websites.

5. **Flickr:** An image and video hosting website and online community. Photos can be shared on Facebook and Twitter and other social networking sites.
6. **Instagram:** A free photo and video sharing app that allows users to apply digital filters, frames and special effects to their photos and then share them on a variety of social networking sites.
7. **Snapchat:** A mobile app that lets users send photos and videos to friends or to their "story." Snaps disappear after viewing or after 24 hours. Currently, we are not allowing individual departments to have Snapchat accounts, but asking that they contribute to the Tufts University account.
8. **LinkedIn Groups:** A place where groups of professionals with similar areas of interest can share information and participate in a conversations.

5.1.3 Key elements of Social Media

There are three main **components** to any successful **social media** content strategy: type of content, time of posting and frequency of posting. The type of content you should post on each **social network** relies on form and context. Form is how you present that information—text only, images, links, video, etc.

Every brand and business needs a custom social media strategy based on their current social media standing, goals, and resources available to them. And while everything in social media tends to hinge on a bunch of independent factors, there are some universal, core building blocks which you need to have in place to ensure that your business gets the most out of its social media initiatives.

1. Social Media Audits: A great social media strategy is built on big-picture mentality - beyond thinking about what you want each individual post to do, you need to look at the overall state of your social media presence before you can move forward. Make a habit of conducting regular social media audits on your channels. A self-audit can help you catch inconsistencies, learn more about what campaigns worked (or not), review benchmarks, and maybe even set new goals, enabling you to consistently improve your social media strategy.

2. Clear Goals: Defining clear goals before you begin any campaign or building a strategy can help you keep track of progress, and identify points at which you may need to ramp up efforts. Focusing on clear goals will give you and your team direction on where to concentrate your energy, and it's key to have a defined focus to unite your overall efforts.

3. Clear Understanding of the Brand's Audience: Getting to know your audience in the most in-depth way possible is also essential to creating social media content which truly resonates with your potential followers and customers. Ask your audience what their pain points are, find out what publications they read, and where they hang out, how much they make. The more you know, and the clearer the picture of your target audience, the better. Figuring out these details will help you come up with ways to connect with and build a more engaged community.

4. The Right Platforms: Here, I'm referring to the right social media network(s) for your business, and becoming well versed in how those platforms work. You should also know that just because a network is popular, that doesn't mean it'll be a good fit for your target audience, or your internal capabilities.

5. A Content Bank and Social Media Schedule: At the core of every successful social media strategy is a solid plan and editorial calendar. Knowing what tasks and important dates are coming up will help keep your team on the same page, and give you the freedom to spend more time engaging with your audience, conducting social listening or taking advantage of spontaneous opportunities to push your initiative.

6. Social Tools: Without tools, all us social media marketers would be going nuts. Effective social media strategies are built on using a mix of automation and timely engagement. Tools can also refer to network specific tools (like Instagram Stories, Facebook Live etc.) which you can integrate to increase your growth on each social media channel.

7. Analysis and Measurement: Every social media strategy should include the measurement and analysis of your efforts. Not every part of your strategy will be a winner, but analyzing and measuring will enable you to stop doing what's not working - and to double-down on the parts that are producing results.

8. Time for Engagement: We're at a point in social media where engagement with your audience has become a key element in growing your network. With so many accounts, posts, and messages being thrown at us every day, we have to make the extra effort to truly become part of the community and put the *social* into social media. A good social media strategy will always include time for interacting, asking questions and connecting with the people we're trying to reach. Also, algorithms take into account your level of interaction when showing your posts to your audience.

The social media landscape is always changing but sticking to the core tactics that work will continue to deliver results. I hope this collection of tips give you a good base, and clarity to get started.

5.2 Introduction to Text Mining

Text mining (also called text data mining or text analytics) is, at its simplest, a method for drawing out content based on meaning and context from a large body (or bodies) of text. The amount of textual information available both on the World Wide Web and in institutional document repositories has undergone exponential growth. But as ever more textual information becomes available, organizations can find themselves hard pressed to obtain meaningful information from huge masses of textual data.

Accordingly, methods of text mining have been created that allow vast amounts of textual information to be accessed and analyzed. Text mining, generally, refers to the work of any system that analyzes large quantities of natural language text to identify lexical or linguistic usage patterns of interest, extracting potentially useful information.

For businesses, the large amount of data generated every day represents both an opportunity and a challenge. On the one side, data helps companies get smart insights on people's opinions about a product or service. Think about all the potential ideas that you could get from analyzing emails, product reviews, social media posts, customer feedback, support tickets, etc. On the other side, there's the dilemma of how to process all this data. And that's where text mining plays a major role.

Like most things related to Natural Language Processing (NLP), text mining may sound like a hard-to-grasp concept. But the truth is, it doesn't need to be. This guide will go through the basics of text mining, explain its different methods and techniques, and make it simple to understand how it works. You will also learn about the main applications of text mining and how companies can use it to automate many of their processes.

5.2.1 Uses of Text Mining

These examples from the Old Bailey Proceedings demonstrate just one possible use of text mining tools - the ability to develop new hypotheses - but there are other uses such as:

1. **Systematic reviewing of literature:** Global research articles increase by about 1.5 million each year and although historians are only interested in a small percentage of those this still equates to a lot of text. Services such as JSTOR and, for historians of the United Kingdom, the Bibliography of British and Irish History, help to sift through that data using search engines, but text mining can go deeper, identifying key themes and highlighting recurrence and the popularity of topics over a period of time.

2. **Testing of hypotheses:** Documents can be mined to see if they confirm or deny an existing hypothesis. In many cases this might be the first opportunity to test an established belief about something to see if a theory is indeed sound.

5.2.2 Difference Between Text Mining, Text Analysis, and Text Analytics

Text mining and text analysis are often used as synonyms. Text analytics, however, is a slightly different concept.

So, what's the difference between text mining and text analytics?

In short, they both intend to solve the same problem (automatically analyzing raw text data) by using different techniques. Text mining identifies relevant information within a text and therefore, provides qualitative results. Text analytics, however, focuses on finding patterns and trends across large sets of data, resulting in more quantitative results. Text analytics is usually used to create graphs, tables and other sorts of visual reports.

Text mining combines notions of statistics, linguistics, and machine learning to create models that learn from training data and can predict results on new information based on their previous experience.

Text analytics, on the other hand, uses results from analyses performed by text mining models, to create graphs and all kinds of data visualizations.

Choosing the right approach depends on what type of information is available. In most cases, both approaches are combined for each analysis, leading to more compelling results.

5.3 Methods and Techniques

There are different methods and techniques for text mining. In this section, we'll cover some of the most frequent.

5.3.1 Basic Methods

1. Word frequency: Word frequency can be used to identify the most recurrent terms or concepts in a set of data. Finding out the most mentioned words in unstructured text can be particularly useful when analyzing customer reviews, social media conversations or customer feedback.

For instance, if the words expensive, overpriced and overrated frequently appear on your customer reviews, it may indicate you need to adjust your prices (or your target market!).

2. Collocation: Collocation refers to a sequence of words that commonly appear near each other. The most common types of collocations are bigrams (a pair of words that are likely to go together, like get started, save time or decision making) and trigrams (a combination of three words, like within walking distance or keep in touch).

Identifying collocations — and counting them as one single word — improves the granularity of the text, allows a better understanding of its semantic structure and, in the end, leads to more accurate text mining results.

3. Concordance: Concordance is used to recognize the particular context or instance in which a word or set of words appears. We all know that the human language can be ambiguous: the same word can be used in many different contexts. Analyzing the concordance of a word can help understand its exact meaning based on context.

5.3.2 Advanced Methods

1. Text Classification: Text classification is the process of assigning categories (tags) to unstructured text data. This essential task of Natural Language Processing (NLP) makes it easy to organize and structure complex text, turning it into meaningful data. Thanks to text classification, businesses can analyze all sorts of information, from emails to support tickets, and obtain valuable insights in a fast and cost-effective way. Below, we'll refer to some of the most popular tasks of text classification - topic analysis, sentiment analysis, language detection, and intent detection.

2. Topic Analysis: Helps you understand the main themes or subjects of a text and is one of the main ways of organizing text data. For example, a support ticket saying my online order hasn't arrived, can be classified as Shipping Issues.

3. Sentiment Analysis: consists of analyzing the emotions that underlie any given text. Suppose you are analyzing a series of reviews about your mobile app. You may find out that the most frequently mentioned topics in those reviews are UI-UX or Ease of Use, but that's not enough information to arrive to any conclusions. Sentiment analysis helps you understand the opinion and feelings in a text, and classify them as positive, negative or neutral. Sentiment analysis has a lot of useful applications in business, from analyzing social media posts to going through reviews or support tickets. In terms of customer support, for instance, you might be able to quickly identify angry customers and prioritize their problems first.

4. Language Detection: allows you to classify a text based on its language. One of its most useful applications is automatically routing support tickets to the right geographically located team. Automating this task is quite simple and helps teams save valuable time.

5. Intent Detection: you could use a text classifier to recognize the intentions or the purpose behind a text automatically. This can be particularly useful when analyzing customer conversations. For example, you could sift through different outbound sales email responses and identify the prospects which are interested in your product from the ones that are not, or the ones who want to unsubscribe.

6. Text Extraction: Text extraction is a text analysis technique that extracts specific pieces of data from a text, like keywords, entity names, addresses, emails, etc. By using text extraction, companies can avoid all the hassle of sorting through their data manually to pull out key information.

Most times, it can be useful to combine text extraction with text classification in the same analysis. Below, we'll refer to some of the main tasks of text extraction – keyword extraction, named entity recognition and feature extraction.

1. **Keyword Extraction:** keywords are the most relevant terms within a text and can be used to summarize its content. Utilizing a keyword extractor allows you to index data to be searched, summarize the content of a text or create tag clouds, among other things.
2. **Named Entity Recognition:** allows you to identify and extract the names of companies, organizations or persons from a text.
3. **Feature Extraction:** helps identify specific characteristics of a product or service in a set of data. For example, if you are analyzing product descriptions, you could easily extract features like color, brand, model, etc.

5.3.3 Why is Text Mining Important?

Individuals and organizations generate tons of data every day. Stats claim that almost 80% of the existing text data is unstructured, meaning it's not organized in a predefined way, it's not searchable, and it's almost impossible to manage. In other words, it's just not useful.

Being able to organize, categorize and capture relevant information from raw data is a major concern and challenge for companies. Text mining is crucial to this mission.

In a business context, unstructured text data can include emails, social media posts, chats, support tickets, surveys, etc. Sorting through all these types of information manually often results in failure. Not only because it's time-consuming and expensive, but also because it's inaccurate and impossible to scale.

Text mining, however, has proved to be a reliable and cost-effective way to achieve accuracy, scalability and quick response times. Here are some of its main advantages in more detail:

Scalability: with text mining it's possible to analyze large volumes of data in just seconds. By automating specific tasks, companies can save a lot of time that can be used to focus on other tasks. This results in more productive businesses.

Real-time analysis: thanks to text mining, companies can prioritize urgent matters accordingly including, detecting a potential crisis, and discovering product flaws or negative reviews in real time. Why is this so important? Because it allows companies to take quick action.

Consistent Criteria: when working on repetitive, manual tasks people are more likely to make mistakes. They also find it hard to maintain consistency and analyze data subjectively. Let's take tagging, for example. For most teams, adding categories to emails or support tickets is a time-consuming task that often leads to errors and inconsistencies. Automating this task not only saves precious time but also allows more accurate results and assures that a uniform criteria is applied to every ticket.

5.4 How Does Text Mining Work?

By now it should have become clear to you that text mining allows you to go further in understanding elements and ideas within a text (or collection of texts) than a search engine, such as Google, ever can. Search engines instruct your computer to search through texts for keywords, but they do not understand the meaning of those words or their context.

The use of advanced searches and **booleans** can help a little, but will still struggle to find, say, if occurrences of 'poison' appear most often with drink or food in the Old Bailey trials. Text mining enables you to identify patterns and relationships which exist within a large body of texts which would otherwise be extremely difficult or time-consuming to discover. Indeed, information retrieval is only the first step, as shown below.

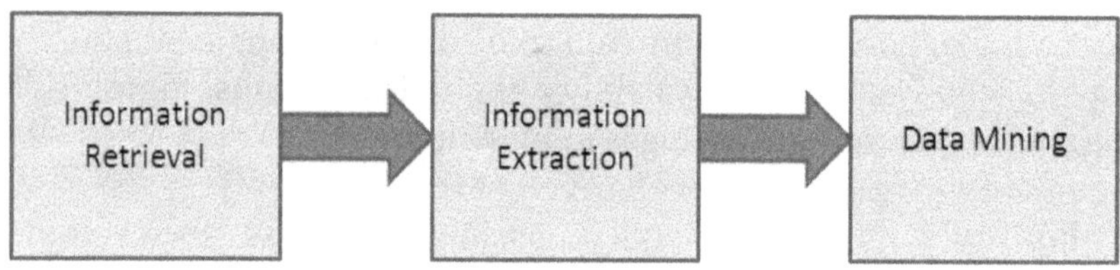

STAGE 1: information retrieval: The first stage of text or data mining is to retrieve information. This might require using a search engine to identify a corpus of texts that are already digitized or it might necessitate digitization of physical texts in publications or manuscripts. This corpus will need to be brought together in a useful format (**XML** is the standard for text mining).

STAGE 2: information extraction: The second stage is the mark-up of text to identify meaning. In most cases this will involve adding **metadata** about the text into a database (i.e., author, title, date, edition etc.), while in others it might involve keying in all person names or locations mentioned in the text (for example). This process allows search engines to extract information and identify relationships between texts based upon the preconceptions of those creating the metadata.

STAGE 3: Data mining: The final stage is to text mine the text(s) using various tools. The purpose is to find associations among pieces of information that draw out meaning and enable researchers to discover new information which might otherwise be difficult to discover. Text mining, then, is a tool that can speed up research and allow us to pose new questions or test old ones.

Text mining tasks include the following similar but distinctive elements

Task	Meaning
Text categorisation	Cataloguing texts into categories
Text clustering	Clustering groups of automatically retrieved text into a list of meaningful categories
Concept/entity extraction	Locating and classifying elements in text into predefined categories such as persons, organizations, locations, monetary values etc.
Granular taxonomies	Enabling organization or classification of information as a set of objects and displayed as a taxonomy
Sentiment analysis	Identifying and extracting subjective information in source materials (e.g., emotion, beliefs)
Document summarization	Creating a shortened version of a text containing the most important elements
Entity relation modelling	Automated learning of relationships between data types

5.4.1 Understanding Text Mining Process

It involves a series of steps as shown in figure.

a. Text Pre-Processing

It involves a series of steps as shown in below:

1. Text Cleanup: Text Cleanup means removing any unnecessary or unwanted information. Such as remove ads from web pages, normalize text converted from binary formats.

2. Tokenization: Tokenizing is simply achieved by splitting the text into white spaces.

3. Part of Speech Tagging: Part-of-Speech (POS) tagging means word class assignment to each token. Its input is given by the tokenized text. Taggers have to cope with unknown words (OOV problem) and ambiguous word-tag mappings.

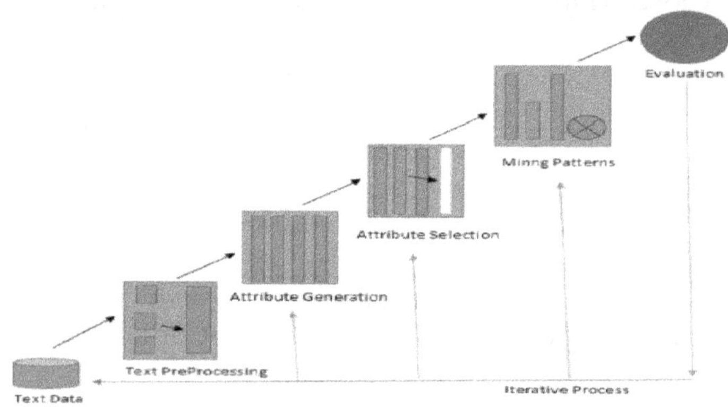

b. Text Transformation (Attribute Generation)

A text document is represented by the words it contains and their occurrences. Two main approaches to document representation are:

i. Bag of words
ii. Vector Space

c. Feature Selection (Attribute Selection)

Feature selection also is known as variable selection. It is the process of selecting a subset of important features for use in model creation. Redundant features are the one which provides no extra information. Irrelevant features provide no useful or relevant information in any context.

d. Data Mining

At this point, the Text mining process merges with the traditional process. Classic Data Mining techniques are used in the structured database. Also, it resulted from the previous stages.

e. Evaluate

Evaluate the result, after evaluation, the result discard.

f. Applications

Text Mining applies in a variety of areas. Some of the most common areas are

1. Web Mining

These days web contains a treasure of information about subjects. Such as persons, companies, organizations, products, etc. that may be of wide interest. Web Mining is an application of data mining techniques. That need to discover hidden and unknown patterns from the Web. Web mining is an activity of identifying term implied in a large document collection. It says C which denotes by a mapping i.e., C →p [10].

2. Medical

Users exchange information with others about subjects of interest. Everyone wants to understand specific diseases, to inform about new therapies. Also, these expert forums also represent seismographs for medical. E-mails, e-consultations, and requests for medical advice. That is via the internet have been analyzed using quantitative or qualitative methods.

3. Resume Filtering

Big enterprises and headhunters receive thousands of resumes from job applicants every day. Extracting information from resumes with high precision and recall is not easy. Automatically extracting this information can the first step in filtering resumes. Hence, automating the process of resume selection is an important task.

5.5 Sentiment Analysis

Sentiment analysis is the process of using text analytics to mine various sources of data for opinions. Often, sentiment analysis is done on the data that is collected from the Internet and from various social media platforms. Politicians and governments often use sentiment analysis to understand how the people feel about themselves and their policies.

Sentiment Analysis has become a hot-trend topic of scientific and market research in the field of Natural Language Processing (NLP) and Machine Learning. Below, you can find 5 useful things you need to know about Sentiment Analysis that are connected to Social Media, Datasets, Machine Learning, Visualizations, and Evaluation Methods applied by researchers and market experts.

1. Social Media are the Main Resource: Sentiment Analysis examines the problem of studying texts, like posts and reviews, uploaded by users on microblogging platforms, forums, and electronic businesses, regarding the opinions they have about a product, service, event, person or idea.

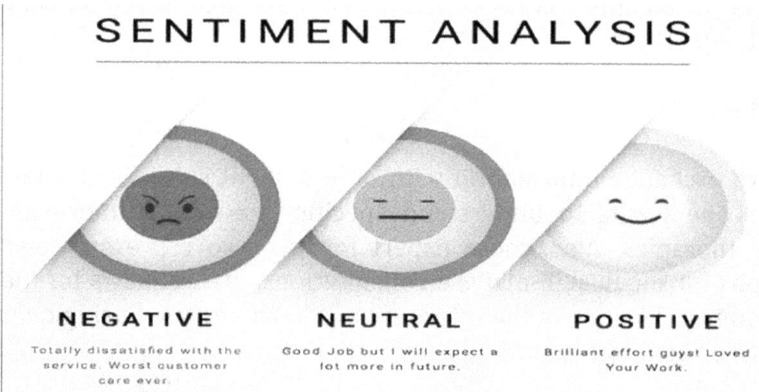
SENTIMENT ANALYSIS
NEGATIVE
Totally dissatisfied with the service. Worst customer care ever.
NEUTRAL
Good Job but I will expect a lot more in future.
POSITIVE
Brilliant effort guys! Loved Your Work.

Classes of Sentiment Analysis

The most common use of Sentiment Analysis is of classifying a text to a class. Depending on the dataset and the reason, Sentiment Classification can be binary (positive or negative) or multi-class (3 or more classes) problem.

In addition, among researchers and stakeholders, you can find either similar or completely different opinions concerning the relation between emotion detection and sentiment analysis, depending on their perspective. However, regardless the result or approach, they all adopt the same techniques.

2. Before Starting the Sentiment Analysis

Datasets: Many evaluations and labeled sentiment datasets have been created, especially for Twitter posts and Amazon product reviews.

The most popular and widespread are:

1. Stanford Twitter Sentiment
2. Sentiment Strength Twitter Dataset
3. Amazon Reviews for Sentiment Analysis
4. Large Movie Review Dataset
5. Sanders Corpus
6. SemEval (Semantic Evaluation) dataset

Also, anyone using the APIs provided by many platforms and forums can crawl and collect data. The most famous API is that of Twitter.

3. Pre-Processing

An initial step in text and sentiment classification is pre-processing. A significant amount of techniques is applied to data in order to reduce the noise of text, reduce dimensionality, and assist in the improvement of classification effectiveness. The most popular techniques include:

1. Remove numbers
2. Stemming
3. Part of speech tagging
4. Remove punctuation
5. Lowercase
6. Remove stopwords

4. How to Classify Sentiment?

Machine Learning: This approach, employes a machine-learning technique and diverse features to construct a classifier that can identify text that expresses sentiment. Nowadays, deep-learning methods are popular because they fit on data learning representations.

Lexicon-Based: This method uses a variety of words annotated by polarity score, to decide the general assessment score of a given content. The strongest asset of this technique is that it does not require any training data, while its weakest point is that a large number of words and expressions are not included in sentiment lexicons.

Hybrid: The combination of machine learning and lexicon-based approaches to address Sentiment Analysis is called Hybrid. Though not commonly used, this method usually produces more promising results than the approaches mentioned above.

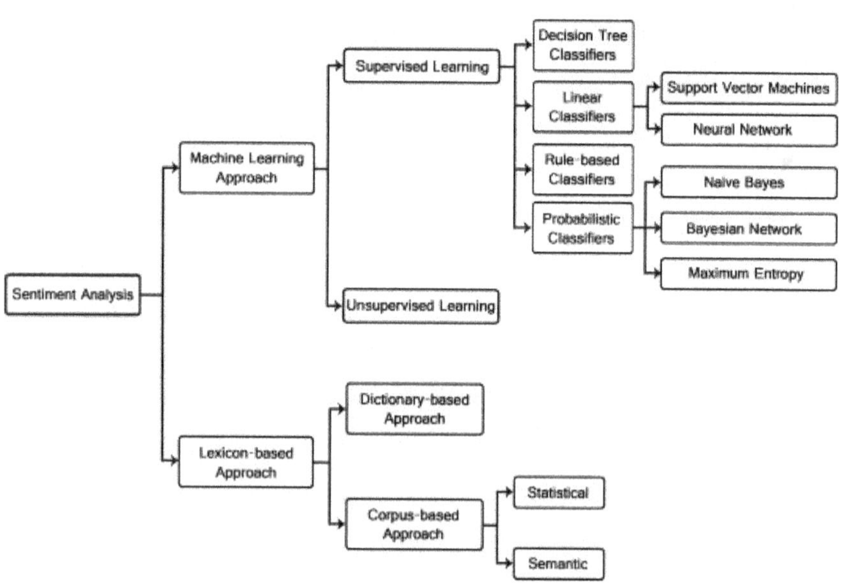

Sentiment classification techniques

5. Evaluation Metrics: As a classification problem, Sentiment Analysis uses the evaluation metrics of Precision, Recall, F-score, and Accuracy. Also, average measures like macro, micro, and weighted F1-scores are useful for multi-class problems. Depending on the balance of classes of the dataset the most appropriate metric should be used.

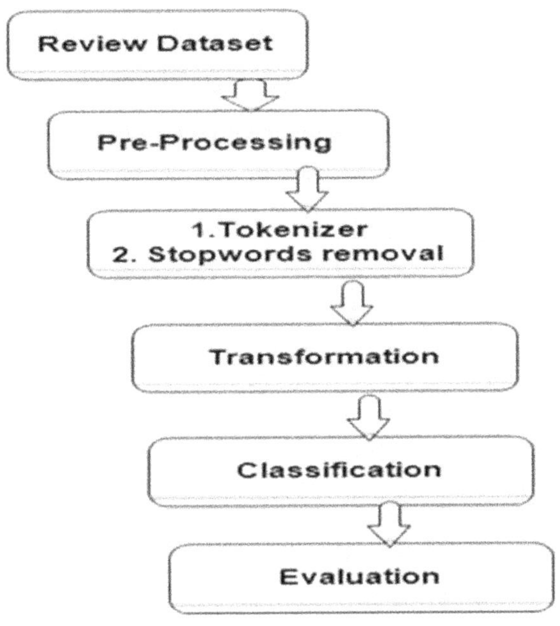

Steps-to-Evaluate-Sentiment-Analysis

6. Visualize Results: To visualize the results of Sentiment Analysis, many people employ well-known techniques, such as graphs, histograms, and confusion matrices. Because of present multiple data domains and tasks, visualizations approaches like wordcloud, interactive maps, sparkline-style plots are also very popular.

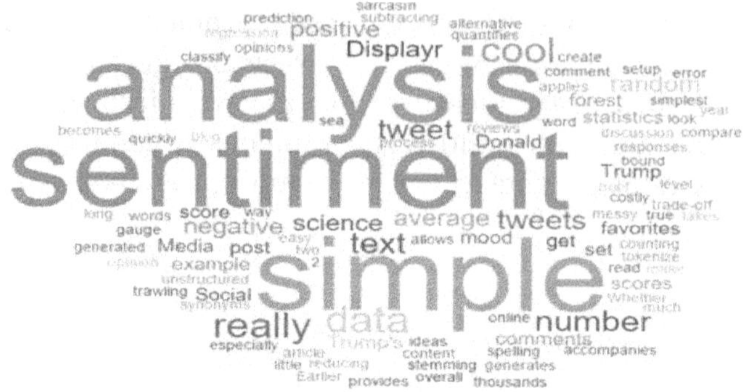

Sentiment Word Cloud

5.6 Performing Social Media Analytics and Opinion Mining on Tweets

A wealth of unstructured opinion data exists online – data that was, until now, unusable. Such data, moreover, is growing all the time. We add to it daily when we talk about our likes and dislikes on social media and elsewhere on the web. We do so in an honest and unsolicited manner, expressing our true feelings towards a brand, a politician, or a global event. The challenge of analyzing these data points on a massive scale has created a new science – that of opinion mining.

In the broadest terms, opinion mining is the science of using text analysis to understand the drivers behind public sentiment. All text is inherently minable. As such, while social media may be an obvious source of current opinion, reviews, call centre transcripts, web pages, online forums and survey responses can all prove equally useful.

Sentiment analysis versus opinion mining: Whereas sentiment analysis – a predecessor to the field of opinion mining – examines how people feel about a given topic (be it positive or negative), opinion mining goes a level deeper, to understand the drivers behind why people feel the way they do.

Why mine? Individual opinions are often reflective of a broader reality. A single customer who takes issue with a new product's design on social media likely speaks for many others. The same goes for a member of the public who takes to a political campaigner's web page to praise or criticise the policies proposed.

Gather enough opinions - and analyse them correctly - and you've got an accurate gauge of the feelings of the silent majority. This relates not only to how people feel, but the drivers underlying why they feel the way they do.

Opinion mining also known as Sentiment analysis refers to the use of natural language processing, text analysis and computational linguistics to identify and extract subjective information in source materials. Sentiment analysis is widely applied to reviews and social media for a variety of applications, ranging from marketing to customer service. The aim of sentiment analysis is to determine the attitude of a speaker or a writer with respect to some topic or the overall contextual polarity of a document.

Opinion mining can be categorized as three different points of view in below figure according to what is emphasized in the research. **The application view focuses** on how to use opinion mining; **the technical view** considers how to improve analytical capabilities; **and the presentation view** uses visualization to improve effective comprehension.

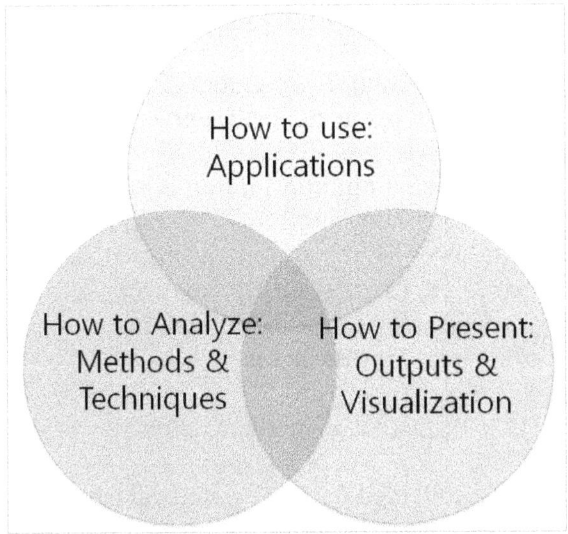

Three Views of Opinion-Mining Research

Studies that researched the application view highlighted how to use opinion mining in business fields in order to discover marketing intelligence and business insights. They analyzed the opinions and complaints of business actors such as consumers, investors, and employees; forecasted movie sales performance; and generated new prediction parameters for stock market investments.

Researchers who used the technical view focused on methods and techniques to find more effective and efficient approaches for improving aspects of analysis performance such as accuracy. They generated moderate algorithms and models, used a specific-purpose dictionary, and applied a new approach.

The remaining researchers used visualization for the effective communication of opinion-mining outputs. They believed that a visual metaphor enables business decision-makers to understand analysis results easily and helps to discover significant opinion patterns. In this regard, they developed new visualization systems and suggested the use of visualized user interfaces and figures that provide an integrated view of analysis results.

5.6.1 Social Media Opinion-Mining Methodology

As aforementioned, opinion mining is deployed to extract, classify, understand, and assess the opinions implicit in text content. Further, sentiment analysis is often used in opinion mining to identify sentiment, affect, subjectivity, and emotional states toward entities, events, and their attributes in such content.

Therefore, a social media opinion-mining methodology should have processes that involve computational techniques to aggregate, extract, analyze, and present the sentiment and attitude of authors in social media content. In this study, we propose a methodology, shown in below figure, for social media opinion mining and conduct this approach into a real business case.

1. Connect to target social media channels and collect data from them
2. Qualify the collected data using natural language processing
3. Apply opinion-mining analytics to the qualified data set
4. Visualize and present opinion-mining results

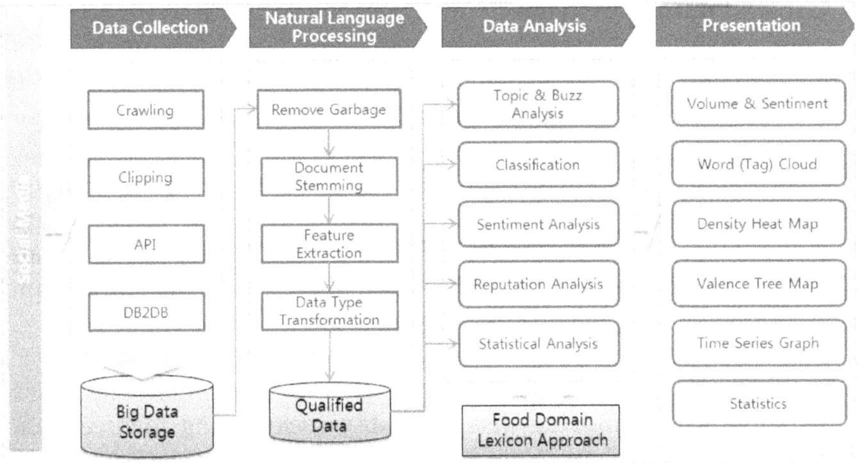

Overview of Social Opinion Mining Methodology

Phase 1: Social Data Aggregation: The first phase for mining social media opinion involves the choice of target social media channels and the collection of data from them. There are many kinds of online communication channel, and the ways to collect data differ depending on the type of social media.

For example, social networking sites such as Twitter and Facebook provide open API for accessing and gathering their data. Portal websites such as Yahoo.com and Naver.com do not support open API but an analyst can use search engine tools and techniques such as web crawlers, web scraping, and search engine robot software programs. In addition, social data can be purchased from social media data providers or obtained directly by applying database-to-database (DB2DB) interfacing modules to social media that allow data collection. Further, because data-gathering methods differ according to the type of social media, the nature of collected data also varies.

Some social media data are stacked as log files in storage while others are managed in relational database. Basically, though, such data are unstructured text generated by users, the volume of which is considerable. In addition, social media are sometimes filled with too much noise such as advertisements and meaningless online emoticons that could distort opinion-mining results. A study had removed ninety percent of gathered tweet data through filtering in the research. If the analyst neglects such garbage data, the results of social media analysis will not provide meaningful and useful business insights. Therefore, aggregated big data should be preprocessed in order to generate useful materials for meaningful analysis.

Phase 2: Data Qualification for Analytics: In the second phase, after aggregating the unstructured text data set, a rigorous data-qualifying procedure using NLP should be conducted. NLP is a computational technique that manipulates, understands, interprets, and presents natural language text for linguistic analysis.

In this phase, NLP is responsible for preprocessing activities: parsing sentences, removing disabled letters, extracting features, and tagging specific characters. For example, meaningless characters such as html tags, punctuation, numbers, and emoticons are eliminated. In addition, stop words, which are invalid words such as prepositions, pronouns, and certain words that are defined as worthless, are removed in this cleansing process.

The subsequent qualified data is then transformed into an analysis data format such as relational data or structured data. The format includes manipulated text and identification information such as created date, author name, content identification, counts, reviews, and favorites.

For example, in the R project software program, social media content can be extracted as list structured text data from a social data file and then exchanged and treated as list, matrix, and vector types. Following this, through NLP the qualified data are stored as a data frame structure combined with identification data. In addition, domain-specific lexicon resources such as a sentiment dictionary and stop words can be generated to improve opinion-mining accuracy.

Phase 3: Applying Opinion-Mining Analytics: The next phase applies various analytics to mine market intelligence and business insights. The qualified data set includes not only information from user-generated content but also various identification data. Depending on the purpose of the analysis, the analyst and researcher can select suitable mining tools. For example, topic extraction and buzz analysis are usually related to market trends analysis, which interests many people.

On the other hand, sentiment analysis is utilized to evaluate the reputations of products, services, and companies, and applied to establish customer responses to marketing activities. If domain-specific language resources such as lexicons or thesauruses have been generated and used in this phase, the analyst can expect more comprehensive and reasonable results. For instance, sentiment analysis results categorized by business domain-specific lexicons can provide a detailed map about the characters that are negative or positive.

Phase 4: Presenting Analysis Results with Visualized Deliverables: The last and concluding phase of the methodology is to present opinion-mining results using visualized outputs such as graphs, tables, and matrixes. As aforementioned, many studies paid little attention to the effective and efficient communication of opinion-mining results to business users.

However, effective visualization is able to explain a considerable portion of analysis results with an integrated visual figure that has no additional descriptions. Therefore, the major focus and purpose of this phase is to make results simple, clear, and easy to understand rather than complex and ostentatious so that business users can easily comprehend their meaning and use them for decision-making.

For example, a tag cloud in topic analysis can visualize topic volume with an intuitive visible font color and size; a sentiment heat map can reveal customers' positive or negative opinions by using two contrasting colors such as red and green; and a valence tree map can provide straightforward visualization by using both volume and sentiment in a hierarchical categorization.

5.6.1.1 Case Study

To illustrate the methodology, we conducted a case study of an instant noodle company, the SY Food Corporation, in South Korea. The market size of the instant noodle "ramen" business in Korea was over US$2 billion in 2013. In particular, SY ramen, a representative product of SY Food, was released as the first ramen in Korea in 1963 and is still ranked on the top 10 ramen list in terms of revenue according to AC Nielsen Korea.

1. Data Collection and Preprocessing: We collected 14,204 items of social media content including blogs, forum (café) messages, and media news articles from January 2012 to June 2013. The collected data were user- generated text content together with author names, user IDs, release dates, URL addresses, etc. This content was gathered from online community websites such as Naver.com and Daum.com in South Korea with a web crawler that used a search keyword of a product name, "SY ramen." The types and volume of the collected data are shown in Table 1.

Types and Volume of Data Set

18 Months	Blogs (Naver)	Blogs (Daum)	Forum (Naver)	News	Others	Total
Volume	5,524	1,647	3,917	1,749	1,367	14,204
Ratio	38.9%	11.6%	27.6%	12.3%	9.6%	100%

According to above Table, the volume of blogs from Naver.com, the foremost Korean portal website, was the biggest in the data set while the volume of news articles from mass media was relatively low. However, the figure shows the movement of data volume along the time line, the volume of news rapidly increased in certain periods such as March and August in 2012 while the volumes of blogs and forum messages were relatively fixed. Thus, it could be said that online consumers revealed various interests and opinions about SY ramen, but media news articles responded significantly to social events such as government compliance and regulation.

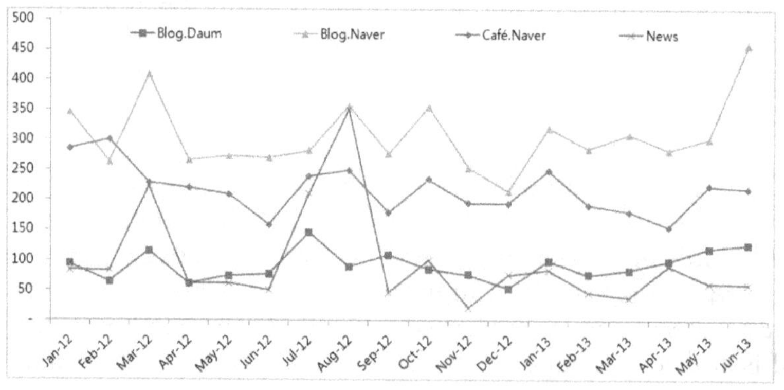

Data Volume by Social Media Source on a Time Line

After gathering social media data, we generated domain-specific language resources such as a domain sentiment dictionary and stop words for the instant noodle business. Since the Korean language does not have a public SentiWordNet for opinion mining, these tasks were conducted by following the opinion-mining model, which generated a domain- specific sentiment dictionary for stock market forecasts.

Next, the qualified data through pre- processing were applied into topic extraction, sentiment analysis, and other mining analytics. Before beginning them, if contents breakdown with subcategories, we can describe analysis results in more detail. In order to achieve a greater understanding of customers' opinions, a study divided features of hotel reviews contents with room, service and price.

Such classification provides a frame that enables closer observation of social media volume and sentiment status from real business perspectives. In this study, we tried to classify the contents within general categories which consist of the four marketing Ps (product, price, promotion, and place), environment, and management of the instant noodle business.

Sentiment Analysis: From this section, we introduce the visualized opinion-mining outputs with a few statistics. The first output, as shown in Table 2, is the sentiment analysis result which reports volume and ratio of polarity: positive, negative and neutral. We can see positive sentiment ratio in whole content is around 26.5% and negative sentiment is about 11%.

Result of Sentiment Analysis

Sentiment	Count %	%
Total	14,204	100.0%
Positive	3,769	26.5%
Negative	1,574	11.1%
Neutral	8,861	62.4%

Next deliverable, as displayed in figure is a simple graph showing the movement in the daily averaged sentiment scores over the research time line. In this figure, the range for sentiment scores is between +1 (extremely positive) and -1 (extremely negative). Sentiment scores are almost all over 0 (neutral sentiment), which means that customers' opinions are relatively positive.

divided the content source into user-generated content (UGC) such as blogs and forums and media-generated content (MGC) such as news article. According to T-test result, in table, there was no significant difference between two sources.

Sentiment T-Test by Sources

		Mean	SD	t	p
Sentiment	**UGC**	0.159	0.138	-0.6936	0.488
	MGC	0.143	0.506		

However, we can find that two social media sources show different movement in Figure below, The sentiment flow of consumer-generated content remains positive and stable area around a score of 0.2 with rare noticeable changes over time, but exceptional dropping points like March, 2012. Interestingly, this period was indeed a time of crisis for instant noodle companies because the Fair Trade Commission (FTC) in Korea imposed a US$100 million fine in that month as a penalty for price collusion among them. On the other hand, the pattern of media channel shows sharp fluctuations from extreme positive to negative. We can consider mass media sensitively reacts to social events rather than preference about the product.

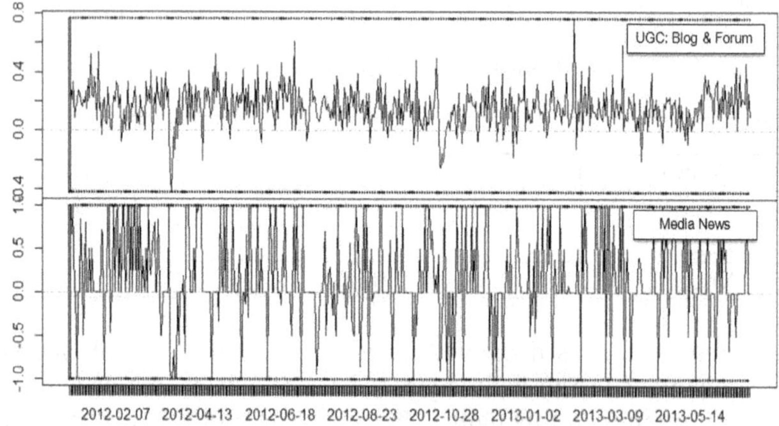

Daily Sentiment Flow: UGC vs. Media News

Topic Extraction

The below figure presents a word cloud (or tag cloud) that extracted hot issues and high frequency topic keywords during the targeted period. The size of a word in the cloud reflects topic volume while color emphasizes the topic. Greater insight can be obtained from this type of word cloud; for example, the below figure indicates that the most significant issues about SY ramen were "Penalty" and "FTC (Fair Trade Commission." This is understandable since the FTC imposed a large penalty on instant noodle companies. Other significant topics were new products such as Ggoggomen™ and Nagasaki Noodle™ because these were highly successful and set new trends in the noodle market. Analysts and business users would expect these to be major issues for companies.

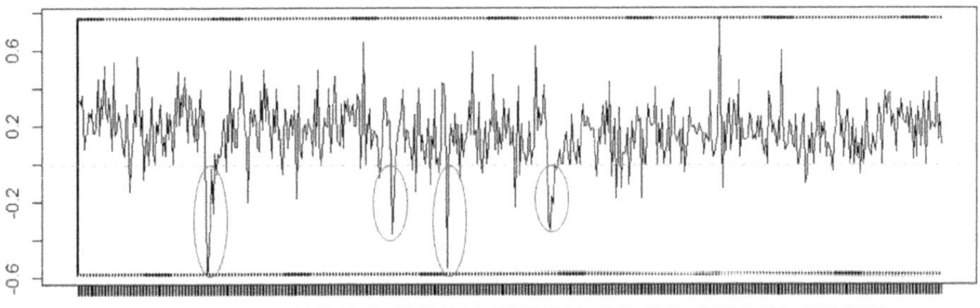

Word Cloud of Topic Extraction

Feature Classification

In the below table, the feature classification result is reported with count and ratio of classified contents; mean and standard deviation of each category; the result of one-way ANOVA test. First, ANOVA test with sentiment score as the dependent variable and feature categories as the independent variable shows that sentiment among feature categories is significantly different ($F = 99.12$, $p < .01$). Comparing sentiment on categories, "soup" feature ranked the highest positive ($m = 0.437$, $sd = 0.637$), and the rest ordered as price noodle, promotion, place, distribution, recipe, competitor, design, top management, material and environment.

ANOVA Test of Sentiment on Category

No.	Category	n	Ratio	Mean	SD	F	p
1	Soup	2,052	14.4%	0.437	0.637		
2	Price	471	3.3%	0.406	0.657		
3	Noodle	368	2.6%	0.266	0.599		
4	Promotion	780	5.5%	0.231	0.602		
5	Place	420	3.0%	0.210	0.581		
6	Distribution	79	17.4%	0.203	0.644	99.12	0.000*
7	Recipe	1,346	9.5%	0.195	0.551		
8	Competitor	2,054	14.5%	0.131	0.613		
9	Design	165	1.2%	0.079	0.492		
10	Top Mgmt	333	2.3%	0.030	0.584		
11	Material	766	5.4%	0.090	0.663		
12	Environment	481	3.4%	0.432	0.712		

**** denote significance levels at 1 %, respectively***

Tree Map consisting of Volume and Sentiment

Heat maps show the density of either volume or sentiment according to categories over a series of periods, whereas tree maps present both volume and sentiment at the same time. Thus, a valence tree map, one of the most comprehensive and holistic visualization modes, can be very helpful for analysts and decision-makers because it enables them to understand the "big picture" of a business situation quickly alongside a hierarchical structure. A simple glance at such a map detects areas that are weak, strong, positive, negative, quiet, or loud.

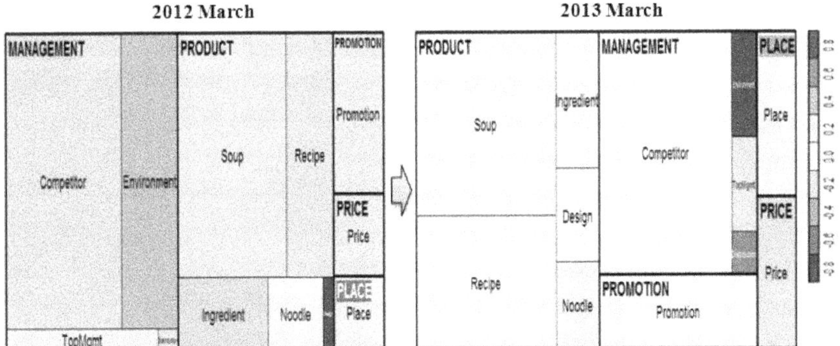

Tree Map: Hierarchical View

As revealed in the above figure, in March 2012 SY Food faced very negative sentiment according to the buzz related to "penalty," "unfair," and "fine" in the management and environment categories, thereby affecting the company's reputation adversely. However, it also shows that the negative sentiment in social media had calmed by March 2013 and the crisis had passed. In addition, the map shows that the most significant interest about the instant noodle ramen is product features such as soup taste, noodle and recipe.

www.ingramcontent.com/pod-product-compliance
Lightning Source LLC
Chambersburg PA
CBHW071201210326
41597CB00016B/1629

9781922617170